English as a Foreign Language

English as a Foreign Language

GRAMMAR AND SYNTAX
FOR TEACHERS AND ADVANCED STUDENTS

By R. A. CLOSE
British Council Representative, Athens

HARVARD UNIVERSITY PRESS
Cambridge, Massachusetts
1962

© George Allen & Unwin Ltd 1962

PRINTED IN GREAT BRITAIN

PREFACE

There seem to be certain difficulties in the learning and teaching of English which arise wherever English as a foreign language is studied. The form and degree of those difficulties, and particularly the treatment of them in teaching, must depend largely on the structure of the learner's mother tongue. Yet I know from many years' experience of English language learning—in Europe, Asia and South America—that the topics I have touched on in this book will be recognised by teachers and students from a wide variety of countries as their 'special problems'.

This book attempts to explain those difficulties to teachers and advanced students. It is not a work-book for beginners. But it is intended to accompany a 'Grammar with Exercises' in which less advanced learners will be given examples of authentic English usage, simple instructions without abstract explanation, and opportunities for putting those instructions into practice on the pattern of the examples provided. The present book works out and explains the principles underlying the Exercises; and it—or something like it—is essential to teachers and students who want to know precisely what they are doing.

'Grammar', said Henry Sweet—to whose *New English Grammar*, as to the *Oxford English Dictionary*, I find myself constantly returning—'satisfies a rational curiosity about the structure and origin of our own and other languages, and teaches us to take an interest in what we hear and utter every day of our lives. . . . Language and grammar are concerned not with form and meaning separately but with the connection between them, these being the real phenomena of language.'

This book was begun in Greece in 1939 and finished there twenty-one years later. That it took so long to write was due chiefly to the elusive nature of the problems it tries to solve. For its beginning and completion in Athens I owe much to contact with a language which traces with astonishing clarity the connection between form and whatever meaning is. However, I owe the idea of it, as well as many ideas in it, to students, teachers and scholars of English in and from many parts of the world, and I hope it will go some way towards answering questions which have puzzled me as much as them.

In particular, I acknowledge the influence of Dr. I. A. Richards, whose work I have followed with admiration ever since I first met him in China in 1937; of the late H. J. Uldall of Copenhagen, of whom I was a colleague at the Institute of English Studies in Athens

7

from 1939 to 1941; of members of 'the Prague School' who were my good friends in Czechoslovakia from 1946 to 1950; and more recently of Professor Randolph Quirk of University College, London. I mention these scholars solely to make it clear where some of the theories in this book originated. For the interpretation and application of any of their work here, the responsibility is entirely the author's.

I am grateful to Professor Bernard Blackstone for reading the typescript of this book, pointing out errors in it and reminding me of other possible interpretations of the problems I have raised; and I am deeply indebted to Professor Quirk and Dr. A. H. King for reading the book in proof and drawing my attention to further flaws. The responsibility for mistakes that remain is also entirely mine.

R. A. C.

CONTENTS

CONTENTS

11

CHAPTER ONE

The Problems

1.   English grammar is first and foremost a matter of fact. We say *one man, two men*; *write, wrote, written*; *he may drive, he wants to drive, no one will stop him driving*. Whoever learns English must accept these forms and constructions as facts, and develop the habit of using them when they are required. Helping us to observe and remember the facts, the grammarian arranges them in a system and draws general rules from them whenever he can. Perhaps he can explain historically how they came to be what they are. In any case, the facts remain, decided for us. *Men* or *I wrote* or *he wants to* is 'right'; *mans* or *I writed* or *he mays to* is 'wrong'; there we have no choice.

2.   Often in speaking and writing English we *have* a choice of forms, each of which by itself is 'correct'. The question then of which to use can best be answered by our knowing, from experience of the language, on what occasions and in what contexts the expressions we have to choose between are acceptable. Until we have gained that experience, we must rely for our answer upon somebody who knows intuitively the right thing to say. Alternatively, we must search for a solution either in the dictionary or in that part of grammar which is concerned not so much with facts as with DISTINCTIONS OF THOUGHT, PERSONAL ATTITUDES, and POINTS OF VIEW. Notice I say 'not *so much* with facts'. There is always an element of fact in the questions we are about to discuss. What turns those questions into *problems* is the element of choice and of subtle distinction which the student fails to understand.

3.   It is this part of English grammar that the foreigner finds most puzzling. When to use or omit *the* or *a*; whether to say *I write* or *I am writing, have written* or *wrote, wrote* or *had written*; how to use *have been* and *had been writing*; how to use *could, would, should, might, must*; whether to put the infinitive or the form of the verb ending in

13

-*ing*; which preposition it is to be; whether to say *some* or *any*, *each* or *every*; where in a sentence to put adverbs; whether to say *say* or *tell*, *do* or *make*; these problems and others like them—whether they belong strictly to so-called grammar or not—are common in the learning of English as a foreign language.* Failure to master them may not always cause misunderstanding. You can often make your meaning clear without using articles at all—for example, in a telegram (see **113**, *e*). Are these distinctions, then, superfluous? Or have they roots that go deep into the thought of native English-speaking people? Whatever the answer may be, they take up a great deal of the teacher's time, and account for many of the students' 'mistakes'.

4. English presents special difficulties in each country and in each different set of circumstances. But the problems mentioned above have risen in every part of the world I have been in. *The exact degree and nature of each difficulty, and particularly the treatment of it in teaching, must depend largely on the structure of the student's own language.* The article, for example, is especially troublesome for students whose mother-tongue has no need for that refinement. Yet 'The articles, tenses and prepositions—please explain them to us, these are our special difficulties', teachers and students have told me, in Moscow and Madrid, in Chile as well as China. These difficulties are therefore not peculiar to any particular area where English is studied, but seem to arise from features inherent in the language.

5. 'Distinctions of verb-tense, and the use of the prepositions and of verbal-groups' (i.e. groups of words whose nucleus is an infinitive, participle or gerund) '. . . are . . . highly developed in English, and are part of the genius of the language.'† In the passage from which that quotation was drawn, Henry Sweet was actually explaining how

---

* This statement is based on my own analyses of errors found in students' written exercises and compositions in different parts of the world, including China, Greece, Chile, Czechoslovakia and Japan. It is supported by the *Report of the University of Cambridge Local Examinations Syndicate on the English Language Paper, December* 1957, which mentions the following mistakes in candidates' answers: 'Inconsistent use of tenses' . . . 'Auxiliary verbs: misuse of such words as *could*, *would*, *should*, *might*, continues to be a great stumbling-block.' . . . 'Gerund and infinitive: the use of the infinitive instead of the verbal noun is wide-spread.' . . . 'Particular difficulty was found when an adverb or an adverbial phrase came near a compound tense.' . . . 'The Articles: errors are common in most countries.' . . . 'Prepositions: correct usage continues to be one of the most intractable of problems; mistakes are wide-spread and very common.'

† Henry Sweet, *A New English Grammar*, first published in 1891 and still worth careful study (Oxford University Press).

tense-forms and verbal groups in English take the place of the subjunctive in certain other languages. Students often attach too much
importance to the subjunctive. They should rest assured that apart
from a few archaic remains it has disappeared from English altogether; and they should cultivate the right use of the tenses, verbal-
groups, prepositions and articles instead.

6. Sweet goes on to say, 'The faculty by which we instinctively
know whether a certain form or construction is in accordance with
the genius of the language or not, is called "the linguistic sense". This
faculty is naturally more highly developed in some people than in
others; but it can always be strengthened by training, and the first
business of grammar is to cultivate it as far as possible.' Now the
problems of English grammar that bewilder a foreign student most,
never seem to bother a native-speaker of English at all. The native-
speaker, though he may fumble over the tenses, articles and prepositions as a child, and though his command of the language may be
defective in other ways, learns unconsciously when certain forms or
constructions satisfy the 'genius' of his tongue. If his linguistic sense
is keen, especially in the way that the linguistic sense of a great writer
is keen, he will use these forms and constructions with precision, in
original as well as conventional phrases. If it is dull, he will use them
imprecisely, in blind obedience to custom and habit. But whether his
own usage is deliberate, consistent and clear, or automatic, haphaz-
ard and confused, what makes him decide to use the definite article
or to omit it, or to select one tense rather than another, would be
almost as much of a mystery to him—if he ever thought about it—
as it is to the foreign learner. The latter cannot help thinking about it;
and, by giving thought, he hopes his 'linguistic sense' for English can
grow. The book you are now reading is based on the belief that to
cultivate this 'faculty' should be one of the main functions of a
grammar of English as a foreign language.

7. The foreign student can ultimately acquire this 'faculty', unconsciously, through the constant reading of good English or by being
steeped for years in an English-speaking atmosphere. More system-
atically, he can develop it by having as his teacher someone who has a
clear vision of the distinctions of thought involved and who illustrates those distinctions accurately by vivid examples. It is very un-
likely that he could acquire it by first being given an abstract explanation of the distinctions of thought. That would have to come later, at
the stage my readers have presumably reached. An accurate explanation of these problems is very hard to formulate; one that is

15

easy is bound to be over-simplified and sooner or later misleading. An accurate explanation would be still harder to follow, especially if the distinctions themselves had not already been felt and seen through genuine examples in their proper contexts.

8.   I imagine that most teachers are well aware of these problems but many are unable to discern the underlying distinctions of thought. Consequently, they find it difficult—perhaps it would not occur to them to try—to transmit a precise picture of those distinctions to anyone they may teach. Instead, they deal with the problems step by step through the application of simple, teachable rules of thumb. That is a sensible thing to do, especially with pupils who will never be able to learn more than the rudiments of English. Teachers whose methods are up to date avoid giving rules directly, but drill their classes in examples which follow the rules they assume to be right. From those examples they expect their pupils ultimately to deduce the same rules for themselves.

The Limitations of so-called Rules

9.   Now the grammarian can draw conclusions from pure and obvious *facts*, as we saw in **1**, and he can call those conclusions Rules. But there are no rules laid down by any authority to guide us in these matters of *choice*; and there is no conclusion about them that a grammarian can *easily* draw. The teacher or student who says, 'Give me a simple but reliable rule for the articles, or the tenses,' is asking for the impossible. Your simple, teachable rules of thumb are not valid for very long. Take three popular examples:

(*a*) Use the definite article to indicate an object of which there is *only one* example present.

(*b*) Use the Present Continuous Tense (*I am writing*) for present action, the Simple Present (*I write*) for action performed habitually.

(*c*) Use the Present Perfect Continuous (*I have been writing*) for action begun in the past and still going on in the present.

I could find hundreds of cases where those rules worked; and could make up hundreds of artificial examples to drill them in class. You could give a series of successful lessons on them. Yet that does not prove them to be 'true'. As *instructions* given at a certain stage in learning the language, they may well produce practical results. Converted into *statements* (e.g. the definite article is used to specify an object of which there is only one example present) they are only partially true; they are generalisations based on one aspect of selected types of usage. Trouble arises when the teacher turns instructions

16

into statements and establishes his rules of thumb as 'norms', dismissing any example that does not fit them as anomalous.

10.   The intelligent student soon finds other types of usage from which one could formulate rules telling him to do the opposite to what he is told to do in 9 (*a*), (*b*) and (*c*). Thus he can also be told:

(*a*) Use the definite article to indicate an object of which there is *more than one* example present.

(*b*) Use the *Simple Present* for present action and the *Present Continuous* for action performed continually.

(*c*) Use the *Present Perfect Continuous* for action begun in the past and *not* extending into the present.

Converted into statements, *these* rules also are partially true (as we shall see in Chapter Three). There is probably more truth in 10 (*a*) than in 9 (*a*), and as much in 10 (*c*) as in 9 (*c*); while the first part of 10 (*b*) might be quite as valid as the first part of 9 (*b*). Both sets of rules, in 9 and 10, generalise on incidental factors that can be self-contradictory.

11.   No wonder the student is in a maze. Many teachers realise that something is wrong, but they stick to their rules of thumb, partly because they have found them to be teachable and examinable, largely because they have no alternative. In consequence:

(*a*) By dealing only with the superficial aspects of the problem, the teacher misses the underlying distinctions of thought.

(*b*) Usage is often distorted to support an easily-teachable rule. The teacher who places his pen firmly on the desk announcing, '*I am putting my pen on the desk*,' in obedience to 9 (*b*), is as guilty as the old-fashioned pedagogue who expected his class to translate '*This is the pen of my aunt*'; while an example like '*I am saying that I am putting my pen on the desk*', taught through faith in the same 'rule', cuts right across the English grain.*

(*c*) Hours are wasted not only on lessons imparting makeshift rules as if they were permanent truths, but also on working out exercises which require the student to choose between two constructions, both of which can be 'right', though one of the two is falsely supposed to be 'wrong'. An instance of this is the exercise based on the 'rule' that *some* is used only in the affirmative, *any* only in the negative and interrogative. Expressions like '*Would you like some tea?*' and '*Any child could tell you that*', which are both perfectly good

---

* See 197 (*b*). The repetition of the -*ing* sound is irritating.

English, are often disallowed because the teacher regards them as disobeying the rule.

(*d*) An elementary rule of thumb will often remain embedded in the learner's mind, all the more so if it was impressively taught. A teacher I know, whose mother-tongue had no equivalent of *a* and *the*, had once been told, 'Use the indefinite article when a noun is first introduced. Whenever the same noun recurs, put the definite article before it.' In support of this precept, he could have quoted Sweet's example: *A man wants to speak to you. I do not know who he is—he is not the man who was here yesterday.* This was his guiding light in any composition he wrote, in every lesson he gave. It led him often aright, often astray. He could never understand why the famous line from Shakespeare's *Richard III*, '*A horse, a horse, my kingdom for a horse*' should not be: '*A horse, the horse, my kingdom for the horse.*'

(*e*) Above all, an inadequate basic rule has sooner or later to be patched up with a clumsy system of sub-rules and exceptions, which may cause far more trouble in the end than a basic rule that is more accurate though less temptingly teachable.

12. Eventually, modern linguistics and psychology combined may explain why—or at least in what circumstances—we say what we do. Their explanation will probably be expressed in terms very different from those of the traditional grammar of Indo-European languages, perhaps in terms very difficult for the ordinary teacher and student to understand. Meanwhile neither the teacher nor the student can wait till the perfect solution is found. So I offer this book as a temporary guide.

CHAPTER TWO

Method of Approach

13. The first thing I would ask of my readers is that they admit the inadequacy of any rule if accepted usage does not agree with it. Though English speakers may sometimes be faced with a choice between one form and another, what they actually say and in what circumstances they say it are matters of fact; and a *general statement* about usage is inaccurate if it is contradicted by the *facts* of generally accepted usage itself. We must not pretend that all usage which fails to fit the rules we formulate is abnormal.

'Dead-end' approaches

14. By the logic of Graeco-Latin grammar, which has determined the thinking of teachers of grammar for centuries, every situation in language must have its Rule, and every Rule its Exception. Now the principle of rule and exception may be applicable to some aspects of English grammar, but not to others. We can establish a rule about the formation of the plural of nouns, and make up a list of exceptions, e.g. *horse, horses*, but *sheep, sheep*. What we cannot do, is conclude that English makes a distinction between one animal and more than one, except in the case of sheep. There is no exception to the rule that English-speakers make a mental distinction between one unit and more than one, whatever the name of that unit may be.

15. Another effect of Graeco-Latin logic has been to make us attach too much importance to the juxtaposition of words. Words do get stuck together, it is true, like pieces of a jigsaw puzzle. But this does not necessarily mean that we use, for example, such-and-such a tense solely because of the juxtaposition of an adverb, as in

(*Now*) I am writing (*at this moment*).
I (*always*) walk home (*every day*).
I have (*already*) seen him (*today*).
I saw him (*yesterday*) (*a week ago*).

What rule does the teacher draw and expect the student to deduce from these examples? Is it: use the Present Continuous (*I am writing*) with *now* and *at this moment*, the Simple Present (*I write*) with *always*, *every day*, and so on? That advice can be helpful, up to a point. Modern linguistics of a purely statistical kind might support it. Given an army of research assistants, or an electronic brain, we could count up the number of times when (*a*) *always* is found with the Simple Present, and (*b*) *always* occurs with the Present Continuous; and then, if (*a*) is considerably greater than (*b*), decide that (*a*) is the 'norm'. *I am always writing* would then be classified as abnormal—although it is something I normally say. Similarly, *now I type my letters, I get up at this point, I saw him today, I know that already*, all impeccable English, could be called irregular.

Incidental and Essential Factors

16.   It is quite true that we form these verbal associations; and it would not be at all surprising if (*a*) in **15** occurred more frequently than (*b*). Yet I wonder how many of my readers feel that this touches the heart of the matter. Adverbial expressions are undoubtedly a factor in tense-usage. But they are an *incidental* factor, not an essential one. When I put on a rain-coat, I usually take my umbrella too. When I wear an overcoat, I feel in my pocket for gloves. When I take out a tropical suit, I start looking for my dark glasses as well. As a habit (and use of language is very much a matter of habit) I associate umbrella with rain-coat, overcoat with gloves, dark glasses with tropical clothes. Let statisticians count up the number of people (*x*) who make those associations, and (*y*) who do not, and argue that (*x*) is the 'norm' if they wish. True, I often put on my rain-coat and then pick up my umbrella automatically. But is it not possible that I perform both actions *primarily* because I know it is raining? Similarly, it is possible that I use the Simple Past, e.g. *I saw*, in automatic association with a phrase like *a moment ago*; but might it not be that I use *both* expressions because my attention is focused on a moment in past time detached from the present?

17.   If such an assumption is permissible, it may help to explain distinctions in usage when incidental factors such as adverbs are absent. In telephoning a busy man one wants to invite to lunch, one might say (and here I quote from conversations overheard) either (*a*) *I hope you will come and have lunch with me* or (*b*) *I am hoping you will come and have lunch with me*. Both are right; but they are not equal in the effect they might have on the hearer. Native-speakers

20

who select (*a*) rather than (*b*), or *vice versa*, may be quite unaware that they do, and unable to explain *why* they do. Any explanation one can offer might be drawn from purely personal associations. My own explanation is that a busy, self-important man might feel (*a*) to be too presumptuous, and refuse the invitation, but (*b*) flatteringly deferential and accept; while someone else to whom that invitation was given might feel (*a*) to be definitely meant, and accept with pleasure, but (*b*) to be uncertain and not sufficiently pressing. The speaker's attitude to his audience—dictatorial or deferential, positive or uncertain—can be an important factor in English tense usage. However, the basic factor in the above examples is not the positiveness, the uncertainty, or whatever it may be in the speaker's attitude, but his conception of the action as whole, or accomplished (*hope*) or partial, in progress or continuing (*hoping*)—see **135**.

18. Since we are concerned in these problems with distinctions of thought, we should look for the essential factors both in the distinctions which all human beings find it necessary to make, and in those which are characteristic of the English-speaking people. Universal distinctions, e.g. between male and female, between one and more than one, will be obvious to the foreign student of English; and the special ways in which masculine and feminine, singular and plural, are indicated and emphasised in English can easily be made clear to him, even though he may make accidental errors in concord. Other distinctions common to many languages, e.g. between completed and uncompleted aspects of activity, or between the act performed once and the frequent repetition of it, will be found in English but indicated or emphasised in a particular way which the student may not appreciate. Still other distinctions may be quite unfamiliar to the student and he may not at first see they exist.

19. A language cannot help reflecting the ways of behaviour and thought of the people who speak it as their mother-tongue. English has developed through the centuries in the daily life of people whose instincts—or whose climate, or whatever it may be—impel them to physical action. They think in physical, rather than in abstract, logical or mystical terms. *They are matter-of-fact.* They like to get on with the job, to get things done, to get results. English-speakers reading this paragraph will want to know where it is all leading to. They are concerned with action, movement, direction, mathematically definite relationships in space. To them, there is an important difference between activity and achievement; still more between the word and the deed. They distinguish sharply between the idea

21

and the reality, the general and the particular, the limitless and the strictly confined, the unspecified and the specific, the symbol and the thing it represents. To questions of fact they want a straight answer; yes or no. They say, 'You know the answer, you remember it, forget it, like it—or you don't.' On the other hand, they are prepared to concede that the answer may depend entirely on one's point of view, on what exactly one has in mind, on where one wants to put the emphasis. Highly individualistic in a close-knit community, they distinguish between the person and people as a whole, between each one and everybody, between the unit and the mass. They see no harm in a man *saying* what he likes: it is what he *tells* to others that may have serious social consequences. From their long experience of acting according to the needs of the moment, they remember what works in this or that circumstance and what does not. Just as they maintain their traditions as helpful reminders of the past, so their idiom is full of sayings and constructions which have served a useful purpose and which they see no reason to discard.

20.   That is the sort of attitude I see reflected in English grammar and the sort of criterion I shall be using in this book. One of the basic characteristics of that attitude is faith in the unalterable nature of fact. My first word of advice to those who want to understand English grammar is therefore: prefer the facts of authentic and acceptable usage to the grammarian's rules. The grammarian can provide the student with rules which will prepare him for some of the facts he will meet, but not for all of them. There is no way of anticipating idiomatic conventions such as *go to school* side by side with *go to the theatre*, or *fail to do something* with *succeed in doing it.* However, I hope that by the time he has finished this book the reader will be able to recognise and form in his own mind the distinctions which have become stereotyped in such idiomatic phrases and which in the living language are constantly at work.

Six Guiding Principles

21.   *First*, both the student and the teacher (who needs to be continually improving his knowledge of the language) should observe what is said and written by speakers and writers of authentic and acceptable English, noting and practising genuine usage in a full context. If they carried this process far enough and thoroughly assimilated what they heard and read, the problems for them would disappear, and the distinctions would come to them as naturally as to native-speakers.

Secondly, they should forget over-simplified rules of thumb as soon as these have served their early practical purposes; and should beware of replacing them with hasty generalisations based on superficial aspects of certain types of usage or on purely personal associations.

Thirdly, they should seek the essential factors beneath the incidental ones. In doing this, they may find many of the mysteries solving themselves.

Fourthly, as teachers they should resist the temptation of trying to explain these things in the abstract too early. Instead—

Fifthly, they should present their pupils with typical and vivid examples which have a direct association with the primary factors, avoiding artificial examples based on a dubious rule. This direct association need not be more difficult for the pupil than the verbal or mechanical association between, say, tense and adverb (which to me is pedantic and dull). Direct association can be simpler and more alive. It can be strikingly impressive if illustrated by film or television showing objects, physical action, and clearly defined relationships in space and time.

Lastly, if the reader has found some neat little formula that has helped him or his students over a particular difficulty, by all means let him use it. What is important is that we should not mistake the tricks that help us at a certain stage in learning for rules that can be applied to the language as a whole.

CHAPTER THREE

Popular Over-Simplifications

22. Before we go any further, let us see what is wrong with the kind of rule quoted in **9.** I am not saying that you should abandon such rules of thumb; but you should know their limitations.

23. *'The definite article is used to indicate an object of which there is only one example present.'* The teacher looks round the room and points to *a chair, a book, a picture*; then to *the door, the floor, the ceiling.* So far, so good. But the student's brow is furrowed when the teacher adds *the table*, forgetting that in a previous lesson he had used the same one-and-only table to ring the changes on the pattern *this is a book, this is a pen, this is A TABLE.* Hurriedly the teacher looks outside and points at *the sun* and *the sky*, thankful that *the stars* in their millions are present only at night.

24. What is wrong? The definite article *is* used to indicate a solitary example. However, (*a*) so is the *in*definite article. Furthermore, (*b*) the definite article is used to indicate the object of which there are *many* examples present; and (*c*) the definite article is *not* used with an object of which there is only one example present. I observe (*a*) when I look up from my writing and see on my wall *a Japanese hanging scroll*—the only specimen for miles around. As for (*b*), in my mind's eye I see a street full of houses and myself wearily walking from one to the other, looking for the one I've been invited to, wondering *which is the house.* In that case, there are far too many examples present. And as for (*c*), if Shakespeare were present at this discussion, there would be an object of which only one example has ever existed; yet we do not say *the Shakespeare, until we imagine that there is more than one example*, and wish, let us say, to distinguish *the Shakespeare we study* from *the Shakespeare his mother knew.*

25. The fact that a Japanese hanging scroll is a most unusual thing to have in one's room only makes it a better example of a

24

unique object. Nor is Shakespeare a bad example merely because the word can be classified as a Proper Noun. Why are proper nouns not usually preceded by an article in English, as they are, for example, in Greek? The article helps to identify one example of a concept, or more than one, and to isolate the identified object or objects from another or from others. In English we do not feel the need for such a device with a proper noun; we feel the name itself is sufficient to identify the object we have in mind. It is only when we begin to form more than one image of the object bearing that name, and wish to distinguish one of those images from another, that we use the article as a signal that we are making such a distinction. *The Shakespeare we study* is in fact a very good example of how the definite article in English functions. This argument will be developed in Chapter Six.

26. *'The Present Continuous (I am writing) is used for present action, the Simple Present (I write) for action performed habitually.'* That is true in the examples *I am writing a book, you are reading it, I write a few hundred words every day*, and countless other examples. But the Simple Present, also, is used for present action. *'I put my pen down at this point, get up, and walk over to the window, thinking out what I shall say next.'* I found myself saying those words quite naturally as I went through the motions. I did *not* say, *'I am putting'* (see **11**, *b*). That would have been either a commentary on a very slow-motion performance, spoken as my hand was gradually descending, or an announcement of my intentions which I cannot imagine myself ever wanting to make.

27. The idea that the Present Continuous is the normal tense for present action has been encouraged in recent years by teachers who have wanted to get their pupils out of the habit of using the Simple Present for every present occasion. Learners who are introduced to the English verb through the paradigm *I write, he or she writes, we write, you write, they write*, constantly recited, tend to use that tense-form too often. Commenting on the uncompleted activity in which I am at this moment engaged, I would not say, 'I write a book.' That sounds 'un-English'; and to prevent or correct that error, teachers have drilled their pupils into saying 'I am writing'. Now the direct association between the physical action of saying the words *I am writing* and the continuous physical movement of hand and pen across the page is a perfect example of what I am trying to advocate in this book. But what many teachers have done is to substitute one error for another—to replace an excessive use of the Simple Present

by an over-insistence on the Present Continuous*—without forming in their pupils' minds the appropriate association in respect of either tense-form.

28. When in real life does one have to comment on action at the time it is being performed? Most of all, in these days, when describing an actual event for the benefit of a wireless audience; also when demonstrating a scientific experiment, a mechanical operation, a process in cookery, a conjuring trick, and so on. In a radio commentary on present action the Simple Present and the Present Continuous may occur with equal frequency. The following, from a television commentary on a mile race, is typical: *Here are the runners—they're†* *taking off their sweaters and moving up to their marks. Ibbotson is Number 32, second from the right. They're off. No—that was a false start. The starter motions them back.* In an observation of the tenses used in a series of such commentaries, it was noted‡ that the Simple Present was used almost entirely in an account of a football-match, the Present Continuous almost entirely throughout a description of the Oxford and Cambridge boat-race. We cannot conclude from this either that the normal rules of English grammar do not apply to wireless commentaries, or that one set of rules applies to football-commentator's English, another to descriptions of university boat-races. The English of wireless commentators may be more alive and more naturally 'correct' than the artificially-systematised language of English-teachers. The difference between the football-match and the boat-race is interesting and will be explained in **146.** As for running commentaries on scientific and other demonstrations, note the following: (*a*) *Now watch me: I switch on the current and stand back.* (*b*) *First, I make sure the gear is in neutral, and then I press the self-starter.* (*c*) *I pour the milk in slowly.* (*d*) *Look carefully: I cut the string once, and I cut it again.* That, too, is natural English. To dismiss it as professional jargon, or as a special case for which some label like Instantaneous or Demonstrative Present must be found, will not help to solve our problems. Nor will it help if we argue that what the demonstrator really means is *Every time I do this, I (habitually) switch —stand back—make sure,* etc. He *may* mean that when he gives a demonstration; but it is just as likely that he means *This is what I do now.*

* The *Report* of the Cambridge Local Examinations Syndicate, quoted in the footnote to paragraph 3, refers to 'the un-English use of the Present Continuous'.
† Such contracted forms represent normal speech, but students would be well advised to avoid them in formal composition or official correspondence.
‡ Noted by Mr. A. V. P. Elliott, of the Institute of Education, University of London.

29. The Simple Present is certainly used to relate habitual action. But that does not entitle us to say that the distinction between the act performed at the present moment and the act performed repeatedly in present time is shown in English by a difference in tense-form except incidentally in certain common types of usage. That distinction is an important one in languages, and it is made in English; but it is best shown in English by adverbial expressions or by the general context. The Simple Present is also used, as we have just seen, for an act performed now; and the Present Continuous can be used for habitual action: e.g. *You're always tapping on the table. Do stop it— it's a most annoying habit.* We must therefore look for other criteria in establishing the essential difference between these two tense-forms.

30. '*The Present Perfect Continuous* (*I have been writing*) *is used for action begun in the past and still going on in the present.*' The exact opposite of the last part of this 'rule' ('still going on in the present') is so often true that there cannot be much advantage in teaching it, even as a temporary aid. The 'rule' applies to such examples as *I have been writing this book for six weeks* (and am still writing it) and *You have been learning English for six years* (and are learning it still). It does not apply to other examples, such as *Who has been sitting in my chair?* when whoever has been sitting in it is no longer there, or '*You have been working too hard,' said the doctor to the patient, motionless in bed,* or *It's been raining but it's stopped now.*

31. '*The Present Perfect* (*I have written*) *is used when we are specially concerned with the present results of past action, when the evidence of past action lies before us.*' There is much truth in this. *Hurray. I've found it. Here it is* and many similar examples would prove the 'rule'. Yet even here we have not found a factor (apart from the form of the construction) which is common to all examples of the tense. When I tell you that *I have lived in China,* I am not necessarily concerned with present results at all. I am not in China now and have not lived there for over twenty years. Evidence may exist of my having lived there, but that evidence would be there just the same if I said *I lived in China before the War*; and I could still say *I have lived in China* though every shred of evidence had disappeared. To take another example: after a worried search for my watch, there is nothing to stop me from saying *Here it is. I found it under the bed.* Note also: *Here is the contract. It came by registered mail.*

32. '*The Present Perfect is used for recent happenings, the Simple Past* (*I wrote*) *for less recent.*' That would be true in some examples.

27

The converse is also true; e.g. *The post came five minutes ago. England has had its civil wars* (the last was in the 17th century).

33. '*The Past Continuous* (*I was writing*) *is used for an action which is interrupted by another action in the past.*' This is part of the traditional stock-in-trade of European language-teachers. However relevant the principle behind it may be to French or Spanish, it applies to English only incidentally and not invariably. In *I was writing when the bell rang*, an interruption is implied. In *The bell was still ringing but I worked on without noticing it* or *Someone was taking notes all the time you were speaking*, what is interrupted by what? *I was writing steadily throughout the afternoon* might mean that I was left completely undisturbed.

34. '*In referring to location,* "in" *is used with a capital city or a town with a large number of inhabitants,* "at" *with a smaller place.*' In so far as this is true, it is a good example of the grammarian's prescription and of conventional usage. I have often found myself saying *in Edinburgh, in Prague, in Tokyo*, in conscious obedience to this 'rule', or to please such inhabitants of those great cities as might expect the rule to be observed for their benefit. Yet the 'rule' is not invariable. An aeroplane flying round the world can be said to stop *at Tokyo, at New Delhi, at Athens, at London*, on its way to New York; and we can say *in* the smallest of villages if that is the world we live in. But let us be careful not to make more rules out of these 'exceptions'. It is a fact (of which we can be certain) that we often use *at* with capital cities on air routes and *in* with villages when we are living in them; but a more fundamental point (of which admittedly we cannot be certain but which would make sense of both 'normal' and 'exceptional' usages) might be that we tend to associate *at* with what we imagine at the time of speaking to be a *point* and *in* with what we imagine to be a *space*, as we shall see later.

35. The reader may come across other over-simplifications. In any case, he can always discover how far rules are inadequate by testing them against genuine and generally-acceptable usage. Rules that break down under that test should not be regarded as axioms, but at best as temporary scaffolding poles which, if allowed to remain, could be mistaken for the real architecture of English and could prevent us from ever seeing it.

CHAPTER FOUR

Primary Distinctions

36. The problems we are concerned with are matters of choice. 'How shall I know if I do choose the right?' as the Prince of Morocco said in *The Merchant of Venice*. Is it *a* or *b*, *b* or *c*, *c* or *a*?

Grammar as a System of Pairs

37. We generally have to select one or the other of a *pair*. One member of a pair may stand in contrast to the other; or each may stand in contrast, in its own way, to some element outside the pair.* As we shall be continually referring to contrast in this book, let us use the symbol *v* instead of 'in contrast to'. Thus we may have *every v each*; *all v every*; *all v each*; *a v the*; *no article v a*; *no article v the*; and many others.

38. One member of a pair can be *marked in some way*; the other *unmarked* in that way; or both may be marked, each standing in contrast in a different way with something unmarked. THIS IS VERY IMPORTANT. To appreciate the principle involved here, notice the marked and unmarked members in the following pairs of words:

Unmarked		Marked
horse	*v*	*mare*
duck	*v*	*drake*
school	*v*	*kindergarten*

Ordinarily we speak of a *horse* whether the animal is male or female. In saying *mare* we are specially concerned with the fact that the

---

* Cf. R. W. Zandvoort, *Handbook of English Grammar* (Longmans, Green & Co., 1957), '. . . we have in English the formal opposition illustrated by such pairs as *boy—boys*, and *boy—boy's*; among the personal pronouns we have the pair *I—we*, and *I—me*, and the set of three *he—she—it*. It is around such oppositions that the grammatical system of the language is to a large extent built up' (p. 86).

animal is a female of the species. In other words, we use the *marked* form when we wish to make a particular distinction, the *unmarked* form when that distinction is not felt to be necessary. Notice that we can say *horse* even though we know the animal is female: in that case, we do not feel the distinction worth making, or it is not there that we wish to place the emphasis. Notice, also, that we *must* say *horse* when we wish to indicate that the creature is male*, not female. We can summarise the matter thus:

Unmarked	Marked
1. *horse* (sex of no con- cern; either sex)	*mare* (female in contrast to male)
2. *horse* (male in con- trast to female)*	

I shall call the first *horse* the *weak* unmarked form; the second *horse*, *strong*. With *duck* and *drake* the roles are reversed: the female happens to be unmarked, the male is the marked member. With *school* and *kindergarten* we have:

1. *school* (for children of all ages)	*kindergarten* (for small child- ren only, not older)
2. *school* (for older children, above kindergarten age)	

39.   The difference between the marked and the unmarked member of a pair is the particular distinction made on the marked member but not on the unmarked; for example, it is the distinction we wish to make when we use *mare* instead of *horse*, *drake* instead of *duck*, *kindergarten* instead of *school*. If you like, we might say that *horse*, *duck* and *school* are the 'norms', the other words are 'variants'.

The Essential Distinction between Marked and Unmarked Members

40.   What particular distinction do we wish to make when we use *mare* instead of *horse*, *drake* instead of *duck*? Is it a question of size? *It might be, incidentally.* Is it a question of colour? Again, it might be. But it is of course primarily one of sex. A distinctive feature of *a kindergarten* might be the smallness of the classroom furniture; but it is primarily the fact that it is designed for children of a certain age.

† *Horse v stallion* form a less common pair. In *stallion v mare* both members are marked in contrast to *horse*.

41.   In the grammatical problems we are discussing, there are diff-erences between one member of a pair and the other which are inci-dental; e.g. the fact that one member may refer to a capital city, the other to a place of lesser importance; that one may be used in a description of a boat-race, the other of a football-match; that one action is interrupted by another; that one member is often associ-ated with a particular adverb. Some of these incidental differences may be more important than others. In any case, what we shall now look for are the primary distinctions.

42.   Below are some of the primary distinctions which seem to apply to problems of English grammar.

ASPECTS of the OBJECTS of our THOUGHT

1. the WHOLE*   *v* the PART
2. the MASS   *v* the UNIT
3. the GENERAL   *v* the PARTICULAR
4. the UNLIMITED   *v* the LIMITED
5. the UNSPECIFIED   *v* the SPECIFIC
6. the SUBSTANCE   *v* the OBJECT consisting of
                           that substance
7. the INANIMATE object *v* the PERSON
8. ONE   *v* MORE THAN ONE
9. TWO   *v* MORE THAN TWO

Aspects of ACTIVITY

10. the ACT as a WHOLE   *v* the UNCOMPLETED
                             PROCESS
11. the ACTION ITSELF   *v* the ACTION FINISHED
12. the ACTION   *v* the RESULT ACHIEVED

Aspects of TIME

13. PRESENT   *v* PAST or FUTURE

Aspects of POSITION in SPACE or TIME

14. No dimension, or unspeci-   *v* one dimension (a LINE),
    fied dimension   two dimensions (a SURFACE),
    (e.g. a POINT)   or three dimensions (a
                                    SPACE)

* What I feel to be the unmarked member of a pair will henceforth always appear on the left.

Aspects of DIRECTION
15. NO MOVEMENT *v* MOVEMENT GOING
OR MOVEMENT
COMING

There are other distinctions which will be evident to the reader, e.g. *male v female, positive v negative,* but let us concentrate on the fifteen quoted above.

43. Examples of these fifteen distinctions would be
1. (WHOLE) *all*; (PART) *some*.
2. (MASS) *amount, much, little*; (UNIT) *number, many, few*.
3. (GENERAL) *language* in the context *Language is a means of communication*; (PARTICULAR) *the language* in *the language (which) we are now studying*.
4. (UNLIMITED) *any* in *take any example you like*; (LIMITED) *some* in *I have some money in my pocket* (it can only be one amount).
5. (UNSPECIFIED) *a man* in *There is a man at the door—I have no idea who he is*; (SPECIFIC) *the man* in *Give this letter to the man who called yesterday—not to anybody else*.
6. (SUBSTANCE) *wood* and *metal* in *Chairs are made of wood or metal*; (OBJECT) *chair* in *This thing is made of wood: it is a chair*.
7. (INANIMATE OBJECT) *which*, as a relative pronoun; *this town* in *the name of this town*; (PERSON) *who*, as a relative pronoun; *your father's* in *your father's name*.*
8. (ONE) *a chair, the chair*; (MORE THAN ONE) *chairs, the chairs*.
9. (TWO) *both, either, neither, between, each other*; (MORE THAN TWO) *all, any, none, among, one another*.
10. (ACT AS A WHOLE) *put* in *I put my pencil down*; (UN-COMPLETED PROCESS) *am putting* in *I am putting it down*.

* The possessive form with *apostrophe s* occurs also in a number of fixed expressions referring to inanimate objects, e.g. *at arm's length, the journey's end, the ship's company,* and in phrases on the pattern of *an hour's work,* e.g. *a day's, week's, month's, year's, two days',* etc., plus *journey, time, delay, wages,* etc. It is used with *animals,* e.g. *the lion's mouth,* but not for plants. *Who* is sometimes used for domestic pets; otherwise *which* is used for animals. *That* (relative pronoun) is common to animate and inanimate things.

11. (ACTION ITSELF) *drink* in *Drink a pint of milk a day*; (ACTION FINISHED) *drink up* in *You haven't finished your medicine—drink it up.*
12. (ACTION) *do* in *What are you doing? Are you busy?*; (RESULT) *make* in *Yes, I'm making some book-shelves.*
13. The distinction between PRESENT time and PAST time, and between PRESENT time and FUTURE, can be shown in a variety of ways in English. The present is the unmarked member in the pairs *present v past, present v future*: we tend to use the Present Tense for all time until we are particularly concerned with the fact that the time has gone by or is yet to come.
14. (POINT, LINE, SURFACE, SPACE) This distinction applies particularly to the prepositions; e.g. *at a point* (i.e. no or unspecified dimension), *along a line, on a surface, in a space.*
15. *Aspects of direction* might be shown diagrammatically thus:

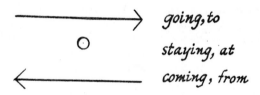

Other Determining Factors

44. In conjunction with these various aspects, we must take into account—

(*a*) WHAT EXACTLY THE SPEAKER HAS IN MIND at the time of speaking. The important thing is not what the object to which he refers is in reality, but what he imagines it to be at the time. '*At a place*' is 'right' if the speaker imagines that place as a point on the map. '*In it*' is 'right' if he sees it as a space-area. We can say *the committee thinks* if we have in mind a *body* of people, or *the committee think* if we have in mind a body of *individual persons.* Both are acceptable, so long as the speaker does not change his point of view erratically. He may say *The committee have finished their work*, but not put *has* with *their*, or *have* with *its.* Nevertheless, in unscripted speech even good speakers change their mental image in the middle of a sentence; but it is safer to avoid this in writing.

(*b*) THE SPEAKER'S POINT OF VIEW; and particularly the point in space or in time which is of primary concern to the speaker at the moment he speaks. The importance of the speaker's point of view is obvious in *here* and *there*, *this* and *that*. It will be found to play a considerable part in tense usage. Notice how it affects the use of *come* and *go*, *bring* and *take*, *up* and *down*. *Come* indicates movement in the same direction as the speaker, or towards his 'point of view' or 'point of primary concern', which might be either where he is or where the person he is addressing happens to be; *go*, in any other direction. *Bring (something)* corresponds more or less to *come with (it)*; *take (it)*, more or less to *go with (it)*. *Up* indicates direction not only towards a higher physical level but also towards a place to which the speaker attaches greater importance, though within a certain area, e.g. a country; *down*, not only towards a lower level but also a place of lesser importance; although these considerations may be outweighed by others, such as *up north* and *down south*. Observe the use of *come*, *go*, *bring*, *take*, *up*, *down*, in the following episode:

(My wife and I are staying in London. The telephone bell rings. My wife answers it. The caller is a friend who lives in the country.)
> *Friend: Would you both like to come down for the week-end on June 20th? I'm coming up to London next Wednesday—let's meet for coffee and we can talk about it then.*
> *My wife (to me): Elizabeth wants us to go down for the week-end on June 20th.*
> *Myself: Yes, I'd like to go.*
> *My wife: (to friend) That's very nice of you. We'd love to come. The only thing is that Peter will be alone—may we bring him too?*
> *Myself (to my wife later) Oh, I forgot. I have a meeting on the 20th. You go and take Peter with you.*
> *My wife: Oh, do come, I don't want to go without you.*

(*c*) THE PARTICULAR EMPHASIS THE SPEAKER WISHES TO MAKE at the time. Emphasis may shift from one part of a concept to another. As in (*a*), a committee can be a BODY of people, or a body of INDIVIDUAL PERSONS. This change of emphasis occurs frequently in English grammar.

How the Right Choice is Made

45. The 'right choice' of construction might therefore be said to result from a socially-acceptable correlation between (*a*) the particular 'aspect' that the speaker has in mind and wishes to emphasise, and (*b*) the construction he selects. His selection may be unconscious

or mechanical, or deliberate. If he is a native-speaker of English, it will most likely be unconscious, resulting from familiarity with 'the genius of the language' as Sweet calls it. It may often be inconsistent and inaccurate. If English is a foreign language to him, he can only develop that unconscious skill through the right kind of exercise, or through plenty of reading and conversation in natural English. Even then he may not develop it at all unless his linguistic sense is sufficiently keen. In any case, he will probably want to know the 'rule' so that he can tell how to choose aright; but to make the right selection deliberately is extremely difficult unless one already knows the language very well. Besides, to be socially-acceptable, the correlation between aspect and construction must be adjusted according to the way in which individual words happen to be treated. For example, *an iron* is a household implement made of the *substance*, iron; but *a wood* usually signifies a group of trees.* Allowance must also be made for conventions which the speaker has to know before he can play the game properly, e.g. the extent to which the Present Tense can be used for future action. Furthermore, he has to know where the dividing line between *general* and *particular*, between *unspecified* and *specific*, etc., falls. For instance, in *War and Peace*, Tolstoy refers to *peace* in general, and to a *particular* example of peace, namely *the peace which followed the war against Napoleon*. But *peace of mind* is not felt to be sufficiently particularised to warrant the definite article (see **129**). We have a sufficiently particular example of peace of mind in *the peace of mind that comes when duty has been done*.

Fixed Expressions, and Freedom to Choose

46. There are a great many fixed expressions in which the speaker finds the right correlation ready made. In natural speech they are produced automatically. Take for example the expressions *to school* and *at school* in the contexts *In most countries all children now have to go to school* and *They stay at school until they are 14 or 15*. In both cases we refer to the concept *school* in general, and use no article; we do not wish to specify the institution—in fact, our emphasis is on something else, namely the education given at school. In the first case we are interested in *movement, going (to)*; in the second, with *position, dimension unspecified*. Now, are *to the school, at the school, in school* or *in the school* 'correct'? Yes, all are if they correspond with what we mean; in other words, if we have good reason for using those

* However, it is also the name of a kind of golf-club, and of a wooden ball used in the game of bowls.

35

marked forms, and if they reflect, in a socially-acceptable way, some special distinction that we wish to make. *To the school* (movement) and *at the school* (position) might be described as marked members of the pairs *to school v to the school* and *at school v at the school*, where we use the signal *the* to show that we are referring not to school in the abstract but to one identifiable school as distinct from another or from others or as distinct from something else. E.g. *In some countries parents are obliged to send their children to the school nearest their home* or *I know Dr. Berry—he taught at the school I used to go to.* Then we have the pair *at school v in school* in which we use the marked member to stress the idea of being in a *space* without specifying the institution; e.g. *You must stay in school till the bus comes to fetch you—it's far too wet to go out.* An example of *in the school* would be '*Every room in the school*' (the Headmaster complained, referring specifically to his own school) '*is overcrowded.*' It often happens that more than one of these phrases is possible in the same context: *Tomorrow is Sports Day, but you must come to school first* (emphasis on 'first') *and not go straight to the sports ground*, or *You must come first to the school* (emphasis on the school building as distinct from the sports ground).

47.   Word-groups like *at school* and *in school* tend to form part of larger groups and to become associated with certain situations. Thus *stay at school* is customarily used to mean *stay at this place called school* or *continue to be a school pupil*, while *stay in school* is used to mean *remain inside the building*. A perfect command of English is therefore said to depend on the speaker's knowing what words and word-groups are commonly used in combination with one another and precisely in what social situation each is employed. There is much truth in that, especially in a language like English where convention and tradition are so strong. But if it were invariably true the learner's task would be endless and English would not be free—as it is, to a remarkable extent—to adapt itself to new situations. The main argument of this book is that the kind of distinctions described in **42** and discernible in stereotyped expressions like *stay at school* and *stay in school* are those that determine free and original usage.

48.   A nice example of an original variant on an ordinary phrase— and a salutary warning with which to end this chapter—are contained in T. S. Eliot's lines

> *The knowledge imposes a pattern, and falsifies,*
> *For the pattern is new in every moment.*   (*East Coker*)

The normal *at every moment* (i.e. at every point in time) would be a lifeless cliché here. The marked use of *in* is evocative, suggesting—to me—the negative of a film in each section of which (i.e. in each separate space) a pattern is slightly changed. Applied to English grammar, the couplet could mean that any system or logical pattern is false from the moment it is established, since the natural pattern of the language is changing continually. No doubt it is changing; but, in essence, perhaps only slightly after all. One could not find very much in Sweet's *New English Grammar* that has been falsified by change since 1891.

CHAPTER FIVE

Aspects of Quantity

ALL, EVERY, EACH, ANY, SOME, NONE, A LITTLE, A FEW, MUCH, MANY, BOTH, EITHER, NEITHER

49.   A clear conception of the function of these words will help the student to understand not only the distinctions expressed by the words themselves but also distinctions made elsewhere in English grammar, e.g. in the use of the articles.

50.   These words stand in contrast with one another in a variety of ways. They form pairs each member of which is marked in contrast to 'no indication of quantity'.

51.   The primary distinctions involved in these contrasts are: *mass v unit, whole v part, unlimited v limited, two v more than two*, with shift of emphasis from one aspect of these distinctions to another. *All v some*, for example, is explained in terms of *whole v part*. This can be simplified to *all v some* : : *whole v part*.

All

52.   Suppose two parcels are delivered at my house, looking exactly alike and shaped like this:

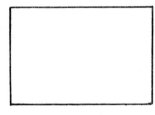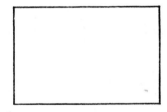

FIG. 1

One parcel contains a large piece of cake, in a solid MASS. Note that it is *a piece of cake*, i.e. part of a greater mass, and not an object

38

complete in itself. The other parcel contains books, in independent UNITS, each a complete whole. When unwrapped, the parcels will look more like this:

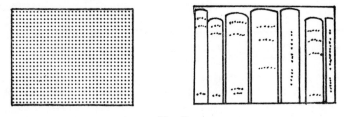

FIG. 2

There we have 'ALL* the 'cake, and 'ALL the 'books. Note: *all the cake—'all of it—is in one box*; *'all the books—'all of them—ARE in* another.

Every

53.   In saying *'all the 'books*, we have in mind a collection of units, with emphasis on the COLLEC-TION. We can imagine the same books with the emphasis on the UNIT. In that case, we refer to EVERY book, and would say *every 'book IS in the box.*

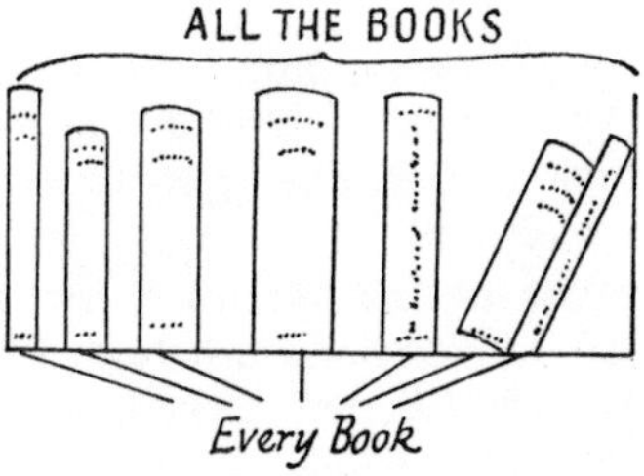

ALL THE BOOKS

Every Book

FIG. 3

There we have *every 'book* or *every 'one* of them. *All v every* :: *the whole collection v the collection considered as separate units.* The double focus in *every*, i.e. the focus both on the unit separately and on the units collectively, often produces utterances like *Everyone was in their place.* This is a very common 'mistake': by traditional rules, one should say *Everyone was in his place*, but that can sound artificial and pedantic.

Each

54.   Let us take all the books again, not all at once, but one at a time; in other words, EACH book. We could, if space permitted, show each book in a series of diagrams like this:

* The mark ' indicates sound stress.

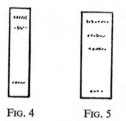

FIG. 4   FIG. 5

and so on, with *each 'one*, or *each* (*each* by itself is used as a pronoun; *every* is not). Thus *every v each :: the units considered all together v the units considered one by one.* Students are often taught that *each* is used for two things, *every* for more than two. In fact, *each* is used both for two and for more than two (see **68**), though *every* is used only for more than two. The difference between *every* and *each* was well illustrated in a film of Shakespeare's *Julius Caesar*, in which Mark Antony was addressing the crowd in the market-place after Caesar's death. Paraphrasing Shakespeare's words slightly, Antony was declaring: '*Caesar has left to every man his fields*' (the film showed us all the people cheering and looking joyfully at one another), '*and to each*'—(pause: the film gave a close-up of one man after another, looking enquiringly and then congratulating *himself*, as Antony went on) —'*a thousand drachmas.*'

Any

55.   Now suppose I cut the cake into slices, of different sizes, and say to you, '*Take ANY of it*'; and suppose I offer you the books saying, '*Take any book you like, any one of them, any of them.*' If you understand English and if you take me at my word, you will choose whatever slice of cake or whatever book or as many slices of cake or as many books or whatever kind of book, you like. You may, if you are greedy, take everything. I am giving you an *unlimited* choice within the whole range; each part of the cake, each book, stands a chance of being selected, thus:

What part, what book, will you have ?

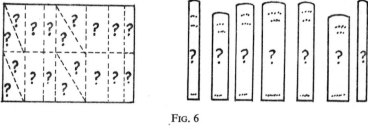

FIG. 6

It might be ANY one

So *any* indicates ONE unit, or number or part or kind, chosen from ALL; and we can say *any cake, any of the cake, any of it, any book, any books, any one, any two, etc., any of them*. In other words, *any*: more than two :: *either*: two (see **68**).

56. In *one chosen from all* the emphasis could fall on *one* or on *all* (see **44,** *c*). Hence a statement like *I don't lend my books to any of the students* can be interpreted in two ways. (In spoken English the difference would be indicated by intonation and stress.) It would mean either *I don't lend my books to one single student—in fact, I lend them to nobody* (emphasis on *not ONE*) or *I don't lend my books to one or more of all the students, but only to one or more of a selected few* (emphasis on *not ALL*).

Some

57. Instead of giving you an unlimited choice, I can divide the parcels up so as to give you one limited part of the mass or a fixed number of the units, thus:

'SOME of the cake

or

some 'cake

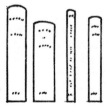

'SOME of the books

or

some 'books

FIG. 7

Put your hand over that diagram quickly. Can you say exactly how much of the cake or how many of the books I have given you? You probably cannot; but whatever the answer is, only one answer is possible. *Some* indicates a fixed though unstated quantity—a limited but unspecified *amount* of a mass or a *number* of units.

58. In *'SOME of the cake* or *'SOME of the books* (*some* pronounced [sʌm]) emphasis falls on the idea of a limited, unspecified part of a particular whole. In *some 'cake, some 'books* (pronounced [səm]) emphasis falls partly on quantity but mainly on the object or objects referred to, without reference to a particular whole. We can also say *'some* [sʌm] *cake, 'some* [sʌm] *books*, with a strong stress on [sʌm], to convey the idea of *one part v another* or of *not all* or *not none*. (In these subtleties, stress and intonation may be as important as the pronunciation of the vowel in *some*.) Similar shifts of emphasis occur in *'all of the cake* (emphasis on quantity), *all the 'cake* (emphasis on quantity and *cake*), *'all the cake* (*all* not *some*); likewise *every* (or *each*) *'one of the books, every* (or *each*) *'book, 'every* (or *'each*) *book; 'any of the cake, any 'cake, 'any cake*; and also with words we shall discuss later in this chapter—*a little, a few, less, fewer, much, many, more, both, either, neither*.

59. *'Some* [sʌm] *book* is also possible and indicates a fixed though unspecified unit, e.g. *There must be 'some* (pronounced [sʌm] with a heavy stress) *book in the library on this subject*.

60. *Some* can stand in contrast to *all*, in which case it suggests only part of the whole, usually a small part. It can also stand in contrast to *none*, when it indicates a positive quantity, which might be large, e.g. *Are we there yet? Oh no—we still have some* [sʌm] *way to go*, i.e. a considerable distance.

No, None, Not any

61. Finally, when every piece of the cake is eaten and every book is given away, then I have NO cake, NO book or NO books left—I have NONE. Notice—*no cake, no book, no books*, but *none of the cake, none of the books, none of it, none of them*. *No* can be followed by both singular and plural: *There is no book here. There are no books here*. *None* (not one of them) is subject to the same kind of double focus as *every*. Thus *None of them knew their parts*. This by traditional rules is 'wrong', but it is widespread. In spoken English, I could say *I haven't ANY cake*, or *ANY books*, in which case I would be giving the impression that every part or every unit in Fig. 6 is excluded.

ASPECTS OF QUANTITY

Some v Any

62. Generally speaking, the most troublesome of these problems is that of *some v any* (see **55–61**). A popular explanation is that *some* is used in affirmative statements, *any* in negative statements or in questions. How far this is valid, and, in so far as it is valid, *why* it is so, may be seen from examples such as the following:

(i) *Take 'any book, 'any books you like* (no matter what the subject, author, size, value, etc.).
   Take some [səm] *'books, 'some* [sʌm] *of the books* (a limited unspecified number, not all, not none).

(ii) *I have some 'books in my bag* (the number though unstated is a definite* one, and here I must use *some* rather than *any*).
   I want some 'books to read on the journey (an unstated but not a varying number or kind).
   I want 'any book or 'any books you have in stock on the subject of flower arrangement (it doesn't matter who the author is or how many books there are or how much they cost).

(iii) *Have you any 'money on you?* (one amount of all the possible amounts, no matter how much or how little).
   Have you some 'money on you? (an unspecified but definite amount—enough, say, for the needs of the moment).

(iv) *No, I haven't 'any (money)*—not one of all the possible amounts. *Some*, indicating a positive quantity, could not be used in this negative statement.

Everything, Anything, Something, etc.

63. What has been said of *every, any, some* and *no* would apply likewise to *everything, everyone, everybody, everywhere, anything, anyone, anybody, anywhere, something, someone, somebody, somewhere, nothing* ['nʌθiŋ], *no one, nobody, nowhere*. Note that *every (any, some, no)*, plus *other thing (person, place)*, becomes *'everything 'else*, etc.

A Little, a Few

64. *A little, a few, little* and *few* could be considered as aspects of *some*, with emphasis on the smallness of the amount or number. *A little* (amount) and *a few* (units) suggest *more than none*; while

---

* The word 'definite', often used in English grammar, can be vague. I use it here to mean 'positive and limited'—I do not mean 'defined or specified'.

little and *few* suggest *almost none*. The pattern is similar to that of *to, at, from* (**43**, distinction 15):

0 1 2 3 4 5 6 etc.

⟶

None ▢

⟵

a little, a few (*Positive*)

some (*Neutral*)

little, few (*Negative*)

Much, Many, etc.

65. The distinction between *amount* (mass) and *number* (units) has been noticed more than once in this chapter. Some words can be used as measurements of both amount and number, viz. *all, any, some, no, none, more* and *a lot of*; others for only one of them:

Indications of

AMOUNT	NUMBER
—	every, each
much	many
a little, little, less	a few, few, fewer*
—	several
a good (or great) deal (of)	a (great) number (of)

66. In short affirmative statements, *much* and *many* are often felt in speech to be too weak to stand alone. Note: *Is there much water in the tank? Not much*; but *There's a lot; there's a good deal*: we would not say *There's much. Have you many books? Not many*; but *Yes, I've a lot, a good many, a great many*.† Affirmative *much* and *many* can stand alone in a more formal statement, especially if supported by a weighty following phrase, e.g. *There is much to be said for this proposal. I see much scope for improvement in the situation. There are many people who never read a book once they have left school.*

BOOK as a MASS; CAKE as a UNIT

67. The two parcels (**52**) might have contained one large book and a box of small cakes. The book would then become the mass, the

* However, the habit of using *less* for a number is now common among native-English speakers.

† Compare: *How far is it to the station? Not far*; but *A long way*. Also *How long have you been waiting? Not long*; but *A long time.*

cakes the units. However, the mass of paper and print which make up the book is restricted by the limits of the object, book; whereas the mass of cake we had before was a fragment of some larger mass. This consideration bears on the use of the articles (see **82**). In any case, the fact that the book can be regarded as a mass and the cakes as units makes it possible for us to say:

MASS	UNITS
all (of) the book	all (of) the cakes

(e.g. *I haven't read all of the book yet—only the first two chapters.*)

| — | every, each cake |
| any of the book | any cake, any cakes |

(e.g. *Have you understood any of the book?*)

some of the book	some cakes
none of the book	none of the cakes, no cake, no cakes
much of the book	many (of the) cakes
a little of the book	a few (of the) cakes

Two comments can be made on this. First, it would be difficult though not impossible to imagine an occasion when *any, some, much, a little* without *of the* could be applied to *book* conceived as a mass. When I say *Have you understood much of the book?* I am thinking of one specified book, indicated by *the*, not of book in a mass undefined. But I could say, for example, *Is there any egg in this soup? Yes, some egg, a little egg,* or *No egg at all.* Second, *any cake* can now be seen to mean both an indefinite part of the mass and one indefinite unit; *some cake,* [səm] or [sʌm], to mean a definite but unstated quantity of a mass, and *'some cake* [sʌm] to mean either *some, not all* of a mass, or a definite unit; and *a little cake* to mean more than none of the mass, or a small unit.

Both, Either, Neither *v* All, Every, Any, Some, None

68. *Both v all* :: *two v more than two.* Similarly, *either* could be paired with *any,* and *neither* with *no (none).* A full comparison and summary would be:

TWO UNITS	MORE THAN TWO UNITS
(a) both, the two (plural) —	all (plural) every (singular)
(b) each (singular)	each (singular)
(c) either, i.e. one or the other (singular)	any, i.e. one or the next or the next (singular) or an indefinite plural number (plural)
(d) one	one; some, i.e. a definite but unspecified number (plural)
(e) neither, i.e. not one, nor the other (singular)	no, none (can be both singular and plural)

Examples:

(a) *Are these two books worth reading? Yes, both are.* [Both of them, both (of) those books, both (of) the books are]	*Are all (of) these books worth reading? Yes, all of them are.* *Every one of them is.*
(b) *I have the two books—one in each hand.*	*I arrange them in four piles—one on each side of the table.*
(c) *Is either of them yours?* *Let me see, either of them may be—either this or that.*	*Is any—or are any—of them yours? Let me see, any one [or more] of them may be mine.*
(d) *Is one of them yours? Yes, one is definitely mine.*	*Is one—or are some—of them yours? One of them is—or some of them are—definitely mine.*
(e) *Neither of them is yours. You can't have either of them.*	*None of them is (or are) yours. You can't have any of them.*

CHAPTER SIX

The Articles

69. The chief problems under this heading are (i) no article *v a*, (ii) no article *v the*, (iii) *a v the*. Involved in the discussion of these is the difficulty of knowing when words should be, or are customarily, put into the plural. We must therefore add (iv) singular form *v* plural form.

70. The primary distinctions which apply to these four problems are: *mass v unit*; *general v particular*; *unspecified v specific*; *substance v object consisting of that substance*; *one v more than one*.

71. Let us take as examples *apple, beauty, child, egg, gas, iron, knowledge, language, man, Shakespeare, stone, sea, water*. Traditional grammar would classify these words as Nouns and subdivide them into Proper Nouns (*Shakespeare*), Abstract Nouns (*beauty, knowledge*, and perhaps *language*), and Common Nouns (all the rest). Modern grammarians would divide them into Countables (*apple, child, egg, language, man*) and Uncountables (*beauty, knowledge, Shakespeare*). They would argue that *iron* and *stone* are Uncountables when referring to substances but Countables when referring to objects consisting of those substances; that *water* is normally an Uncountable, though exceptionally it is Countable in literary, archaic or proverbial expressions such as *Still waters run deep*; that *sea* on the other hand is Countable, although we commonly talk of *the sea* (singular); and that *gas* is Uncountable, except when it refers to a *kind* of gas. These classifications have been used to formulate 'rules' for the articles, thus:

(*a*) Proper Nouns do not take articles; e.g. *Shakespeare was a poet.*

(*b*) Abstract Nouns do not take *a* or *an*, and only take *the* when followed by a restricting phrase or when such a phrase is understood; e.g. *Knowledge can be dangerous without wisdom. Everybody wants peace. Beauty is skin deep. Switzerland is famous for the beauty of its mountain scenery.*

(c) Countable Nouns take *a* in the singular and can be put into the plural. Uncountable Nouns do not take *a* and cannot have a plural form.

72.   These classifications and 'rules' may be useful in teaching. But they work only within certain limits, and it is beyond these limits that troubles arise. To begin with, *apple, beauty, child,* etc., are WORDS; and the distinctions we are discussing in this book apply *not to mere words* but to *what we have in mind when we use them.* Moreover, English words as used today no longer fit exactly into the traditional categories of Indo-European grammar. If *iron* is a noun, it also acts as an adjective and a verb, as any good dictionary would confirm. *Beauty* can be called 'abstract'; but its use as a Common Noun is now familiar. *A beauty* could be a beautiful woman, or a fine specimen or anything; and, in the spirit of the language, other Abstract Nouns could 'behave' in a similar way. Moreover, we can think of *man* in the abstract, in spite of its being a Common Noun. Classification into Countable and Uncountable is also of limited validity. Examine the statement *Egg is a Countable Noun.* The one WORD *egg* is *un*countable. So is the one word *eggs.* Two words or more—*egg* or *eggs*—are countable. The THING, egg, is uncountable. Eggs (THINGS) are countable. Egg, the SUBSTANCE, is presumably uncountable, in which case the word describing it takes no article. Note:

Grandmother	*I know what you had for breakfast this morning.*
Grandchild	*What did I have then?*
Grandmother	*Egg.*
Grandchild	*How do you know?*
Grandmother	*Because you have egg on your chin.*
Grandchild	*Well, you're wrong. I had egg yesterday.*

On the other hand, *money* is called an Uncountable, although the counting of money must be one of the commonest of human activities.

73.   The concepts of Abstract and Proper Nouns are so important in general education that it is worth teaching them for their own sake. They are helpful but not essential in understanding the problems set out in **69**. More relevant to our problems is the distinction between countable and uncountable, though as we saw in **72** the terms Countable Nouns and Uncountable Nouns are inaccurate.* I shall

---

* They can, however, prove convenient, so long as the teacher realises their limitations.

therefore treat *apple*, *beauty*, *child*, *egg*, etc., less in terms of Abstract, Proper, Countable and Uncountable Nouns, which may be better known to the reader, than in terms of the distinctions given in **70**.

The Noun Unmarked—without Article

74.   In a set of pictures designed for teaching reading to English-speaking children, I found one like this:

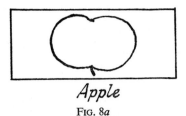

Apple

FIG. 8*a*

The children were supposed to copy this picture, filling a whole page with 'apple' and writing APPLE at the bottom. Note the caption—a genuine use of English by a famous teacher-training college in Edinburgh: it was not 'AN APPLE' or 'THE APPLE' but simply 'APPLE'. The need for the special distinction indicated by the articles was presumed not yet to have arisen. The child's mind was not to be confused by the possibility of there being other apples, of other things from which the one he was drawing needed to be distinguished. The thing he was drawing filled the picture.

75.   Take another example. According to an ancient story, before men began presumptuously to build the Tower of Babel so that they could climb up to Heaven, they spoke one tongue. The idea of other languages had never occurred to them. In such a situation we would say, 'Men used language to speak with one another,' just as we can still say, 'Man is superior to the animals in that he uses language to convey his thoughts.' Let us represent 'language' thus:

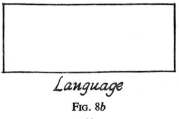

Language

FIG. 8*b*

49

The Noun Marked to Suggest an Unlimited Collection of Units

76. Later in the set of pictures mentioned in **74**, this illustration was provided:

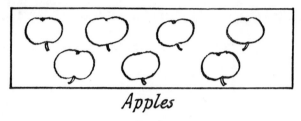

Apples

FIG. 9*a*

The picture contained, as it happened, seven apples. But the object of the exercise was not to teach infants to count, it was simply to present them with a picture filled with **APPLES** and to let them copy it. Happily, they went on drawing apples till their page was full. Then they copied the word itself.

77. The story of Babel goes on to tell us that as a punishment for their presumption men were made to speak different languages. Fig. 8(b) then becomes:

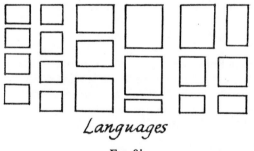

Languages

FIG. 9*b*

78. A film or television camera could move away from Fig. 8(a) in order to produce Fig. 9(a)—telescopically as it were. It could take a *close-up* of Fig. 8(b) in order to produce Fig. 9(b)—microscopically. The whole sequence of this argument (**74** to **96** inclusive) could lend itself very well to treatment by animated film. Note that if Fig. 8(b) represented a mass of **WATER**, the camera moving towards it

would show a smaller area of water; away from it, a larger area: but it *would not show water as units.*

79.   In Fig. 8(a) and 8(b) we are dealing with an unmarked form; with an undivided whole; a mass; the concept in general; an example of the concept not distinguished from other examples of the same concept or from different concepts; the concept that fills the picture. In Fig 9(a) and 9(b) we are using a marked form in which we are particularly concerned with the two concepts in terms of UNITS— with APPLES or LANGUAGES in general. The choice of *apple v apples* or *language v languages* is therefore a matter of *mass in general v units in general*; but see **84.**

The Noun Marked with A or AN

80.   Select any ONE of the units in Fig. 9(a) or 9(b). Now you have one complete example of the concept—AN APPLE or A LAN- GUAGE. You can make up Fig. 10(a) and Fig. 10(b) for yourself by writing AN APPLE or A LANGUAGE under each one of the units in Fig. 9(a) and Fig. 9(b). We could express *apple v an apple* as *concept in general v one complete, independent but unspecified example of it. An* (before a vowel-sound) and *a* (before a consonant-sound) might be considered as unemphasised forms of *one*: they have a very weak stress, and a weak pronunciation [ən, ə]. In the pair *a* (or *an*) *v one* we use the marked form to stress the idea of 'one and not more than one', or 'one and not another'; e.g. *There is only 'one apple left—there were plenty this morning,* or *One man's meat is another man's poison.* We also use *one* as a pronoun, e.g. *Will you have an apple? Thank you, I have one,* i.e. I have an apple. Notice also *One day (as we were sitting quietly in the garden)* . . . i.e. on a definite but unspecified day (cf. *some,* **59**).

81.   Note that *an apple* is one of all the things called by that name, i.e. one of a class. In that formula, *one of a class,* the emphasis can fall on *quantity* (one) or on *class* (see **44,** *c*). We may be concerned either with *one thing* in the class, e.g. *I'm not hungry—all I want is an apple,* or with something *in that class and in no other,* e.g. *An apple is a kind of fruit,* and *That's not an apple, it's a pear.* This may be important when the student compares the use of *a* with the corresponding device in his own language, and when he comes to the plural of the article in English (see **84**).

82.   Note also that *a language* is an independent whole. It is a

51

finished product; it is not merely a fragment or sample, which we would still call *language*, without the article. This sentence contains 'language', by which I mean 'a sample of language': here I do not mean 'language in general'; although we use the same expression (*language*, without article) to express both meanings. Likewise, a fragment or sample of 'apple' is simply *apple*; this explains the use of *egg* in the anecdote in **72**. However, if we are concerned with the size of the fragment or the volume of the part, we would use a modifier like *some*. Compare *This is water* (class) and *May I have some water?* (quantity, as well as class). The shift of emphasis here is comparable to that in **81**.

83. *A* is by tradition called 'the indefinite article'. It can in fact indicate both an indefinite unit (*I want a pencil—any one will do*) or a definite one (*There was a man—or some* [sʌm] *man—enquiring for you while you were out*). A better term for *a* (*an*) might be the *non-specifying article*. The non-specifying article is either quantitative or classifying (**81**), and applies only to a complete unit (**82**).

The Plural of 'an apple', 'a language'

84. Next, pick out MORE THAN ONE of the units in Fig. 9(a) and Fig. 9(b), and you have APPLES and LANGUAGES. This is the same form as for Fig. 9 as a whole, and explains why the one word *languages* could be translated into French, for example, in two different ways, viz. *les langues* (languages in general), *des langues* (more than one). To express the idea of 'more than one' (cf. **81** and **82**), we usually give some indications of quantity by means of a number or an expression like *some, a few, a lot of*; e.g. *Is there anything else you want, Madam? Yes, I want some eggs, please.* However, in *These are apples, not pears*, or *Would you like eggs for breakfast, or something else?* our principal concern is with class.

The Noun marked with THE

85. Select one of the units from Fig. 9 again. Which one have you chosen? THIS one, indicated by some gesture. (Or THAT one: whether you call it 'this' or 'that' depends on your point of view.) In any case, we are now concerned with a specified unit—this one (or that one) which you have chosen, and no other. Let us put a mark on it, or a line round it, to distinguish it from the rest. There is THE APPLE. Which one? This one (or that one) which we are talking about, and not any of the others.

This is THE APPLE

FIG. 11

Once the unit has been identified *the* serves as a weak form of *this* or *that*, and makes it unnecessary for these words to be repeated with the unit in question. Note that *this* and *that* are felt to be sufficient by themselves to indicate the thing we are talking about; so are *these, those, my, your, his, her, its, our, their*, and a name in the possessive form coming before a noun, e.g. *Napoleon's hat*. These words are therefore not accompanied by *the*, as they would be in a literal translation from some languages. On the other hand, *the* is not sufficient by itself to identify the unit. It functions as a *signal of specification*, the actual identification being provided either by some restricting word or phrase which makes it clear which thing we mean, *or by the context*. If I say *Take the apple*, I assume you know, from the context or situation, which apple I am referring to: in this case, it is the one you have chosen and no other. Notice also that while *this* and *that* can be used as pronouns, *the* cannot. In avoiding the repetition of the noun, we should have to say *Take this (one) or that (one), take the one you have chosen*; or, in a weaker form, *Take it*. It is worth noting here that *this* and *that* have relatively strong stresses in speech, whereas *the* and *it* are stressed very lightly.*

86.   Now if all the units in Fig. 11, except the one marked, were fruit other than apples, then in saying *Take the apple* I would be specifying that object called an apple as distinct from objects not belonging to that class. And if all the objects in Fig. 11 were taken away except the one marked, so that there was only one object in front of us, namely an apple, then in saying *Take the apple*, I would obviously be specifying that object. This explains why *the* appears to perform different functions, though its basic function is always the same.

* *The* is given a strong stress in an example like "Is that *the* Shakespeare?" i.e. the one we all know, or is it somebody else with the same name? In that case, *the* is pronounced [ði:], whereas normally it is [ðə] before a consonant-sound, [ði] before a vowel-sound.

87.   The functions of *the* might be demonstrated as follows:

X

This is an X. (Note there is only one.)

(*a*) X [X]   or   X X [X] X
The same X, marked to distinguish it from
another X or from other X's.

(*b*) Y [X] Z   or   Y Z [X] Y Z
The X, marked to distinguish it from a Y or a Z,
or from Y's or Z's.

(*c*)   [X]
the X—it is perfectly clear which one I mean.

In (*a*) and (*b*) we could also say *The X as distinct from THE other X or from THE Y, etc.*, since it is clear from the diagram which other X, etc., is meant.

88.   In **87** (*a*), the emphasis is on *that member of a class* as distinct from others of the same class; and here the function of *the* is to signal specification within a class. In **87** (*b*), the emphasis is on *that class* as distinct from another class or from other classes; and here the function is to signal specification between classes. In **87** (*c*), the emphasis is on *that member*; and here the function is to specify an object which, *in the context*, stands as the solitary example of its kind.

89.   'The solitary example present of its kind' can bear a mark of distinction in a double sense: it is distinguished from other things by its solitariness, and it can acquire distinction in the sense of 'prestige'. This is noticeable in *the King, the Headmaster, the Rector, the Laird, the MacDonald* (the chief of the MacDonald Clan), *the kilt* (that special kind of garment, regarded by the Scots with pride).

90.   The three categories in **87** are marked by differences of stress noticeable when the noun is preceded by an adjective; thus:

(a) *Which will you have, the 'red apple or the 'green one?* (Stress on the adjectives, *red* and *green*.)

(b) *The young 'student often thinks he knows more than the experienced 'teacher.* (Stress on the *nouns*.)

(c) *The dis'tinguished 'President of our country. The 'blue 'sea.* (Stress on both adjectives and nouns, more or less equally.)

91.   There is another way of looking at **87** (*c*). If we consider the separate parts of what is in the square in **87**, we see that a certain point in the pattern is picked out from the rest. In other words, some object, some point in space, is specially marked. Imagine that the square contains a plan of your room or of your house, or a map of the district you live in; and that X represents a specified object in the room, or part of your house, or place in the town. In referring to that object or whatever it may be, you and the person you are addressing may know that other objects of the same class exist, but you and he know perfectly well which one you have in mind. In English, we are constantly referring to definite, marked objects and places on the map of our domestic, social and personal experience. Thus, on the plan of my room I indicate *the door, the floor, the ceiling, the fire-place;* of my house, *the kitchen, the dining-room, the stairs, the bathroom;* of the ground where my house stands, *the garden, the lawn;* of the surroundings, *the road, the pavement;* of the district I live in, *the post-office, the grocer's, the bank, the railway station, the church, the school, the theatre, the market;* beyond, *the country, the sea, the sky.* I do not give these objects an exclusive name, such as *London;* I use a name that can be applied to other objects of the same kind.

92.   Examples of **87** (*a*) are:
Here are two apples: you may have the 'bigger one.
Here are three: we'll cut the 'biggest in half.

Examples of 87 (*b*):
Which is heavier, this 'egg or this 'stone? The 'stone.
The 'lion (an imaginary representative of a class, as distinct from animals of other classes) *is the king of beasts.*
The (imaginary) *'student, as distinct from the* (imaginary) *'teacher.*

Examples of **87** (*c*):
The table—the one I am writing at. *The ceiling*—the ceiling of this room. *The President* (of our country) *will arrive at half past two. The student* (the imaginary class-representative we keep talking about). *The sun* (the sun we all know) *sets in the west.*

The specification, for which *the* prepares the hearer or reader, is provided in (*a*) by *bigger* and *biggest*; in (*b*) by the line of distinction drawn or imaginable in the context between one class of object and another or others; and in (*c*) by the assumption that the hearer knows which particular object is named by the class-word.

93. Whichever way one looks at it, therefore, *a v the* is a question of *unspecified unit v unit specified in the context, or assumed by the speaker to be identifiable by the hearer.*

94. Similarly THE LANGUAGE would be a specified, complete example of language, e.g. *the English language.* However, it could also refer to a *specified* fragment or sample (see **82**); thus *I hope the language I am using now is not too obscure* or *The egg on the child's chin* (**72**) *had come from the breakfast he had eaten the day before.*

THE with the Plural Form of the Noun

95. THE APPLES, THE LANGUAGES, can then be explained as specified *units*, corresponding to THESE or THOSE APPLES, etc. The pronoun in the plural would be *Take these, or those. Take the ones you have chosen. Take them.* Changes of emphasis would occur as in **87**. Thus, an example of **87** (*a*) in the plural would be *These are not the apples I ordered*; of **87** (*b*) *Divide the sheep from the goats* or *The British Isles are inhabited by the English, the Scots, the Welsh, and the Irish*; **87** (*c*) *the stars are very clear tonight*, or *Where do you spend the summer—by the sea or in the mountains?*

96. We do not, however, use the plural form, *the apples*, etc., for specified fragments; cf. **94**. To express this idea, we should have to say, for example, *the pieces of apple, the kinds of language, the drops of water*, and so on. This introduces what I shall call 'classifiers' and discuss under that name in **110**.

Summary of use of article

97. We could now make up a complete 'declension' for nouns and articles in modern English as follows:

Case 1. apple	language	—the concept in general; the mass, or sample of a mass; the unmarked form.

Case 2. apples	languages	—the concept in general seen as a collection of complete units.
Case 3. an apple	a language	—one, complete, unspecified unit and example of the concept.
Case 4. apples	languages	—more than one unspecified unit.
Case 5. the apple	the language	—one example, either complete unit or sample, assumed by the speaker to be identifiable by the hearer.
Case 6. the apples	the languages	—more than one identifiable unit.

98.   Potentially, every noun in English could occupy all of these six positions. In practice, because of the nature of the things we talk about, because of the native-English speaker's conception of them, for historical reasons, or simply because of fashion, some nouns fill all six positions more easily and frequently than others do. *Stone*, the substance from which buildings and statues are made, fits into Case 1; *stone*, the sharply-defined object that one can pick up and throw, fills the other five cases. *Gas* is sufficiently nebulous for the concept in general; *a gas* as an independent unit is harder to visualise than *a stone*, yet it is common enough in chemistry. An example of *child* in Case 1 would be difficult to find (perhaps for the reason suggested in **118**), although *man* is familiar (see the example in **75**). We talk of *a knowledge of Russian*; but *knowledges* is a potential rather than an actual usage and the foreign student would be wiser to leave it for a native-English writer to experiment with. *Shakespeares* would be less rare, since many countries aspire to have their own.

99.   In common practice—and this is a useful starting point for the teacher—we tend to form three 'declensions', composed of:
(i)   *Special Names* (or Proper Nouns). In the main, these occur only in Case 1, since with special names the need for making the distinctions contained in the other five cases does not normally arise. Example: *Shakespeare*.
(ii)   *Words denoting substances* (solid or liquid) *and abstractions which cannot easily be seen* (by English-speaking people at least) *to form themselves into separate, complete units*. These occur mostly in Case 1; and in Case 5 when a specified fragment or sample is referred to. Examples: Case 1—*Water is heavier than air*. Case 5—*The water*

here is excellent. Words in this category might be called *mass-words* (or 'uncountables').

(iii) *Words denoting things* (animate or inanimate) *which are usually imagined as separate, complete units,* and as members of a class. These commonly occur in all the cases *except* Case 1; thus—

Case 2. *Apples grow on trees.*
Case 3. *This is an apple. Here is an apple.*
Case 4. *These are apples. Here are some apples.*
Case 5. *This is the apple mentioned in Case 3.*
Case 6. *These are the apples mentioned in Case 4.*

Words in this category might be called *unit-words* (or 'countables'). Certain of the things represented by these words, however, are known to us normally as solitary members of their class, e.g. *the sun, the moon, the sea, the sky,* and these words would first occur to our minds in Case 5.

100. The dividing line between these categories is not always easy to draw. Is *breakfast,* in *Breakfast is at eight,* a unit-word used as a mass-word; or is it *vice-versa,* in *I ate an enormous breakfast this morning*? The difficulty of drawing the line, as well as the fact that there is a line to be drawn, emerges from the following test: Apply the question *What is . . .?* to the words taken as examples in the first sentence of **71.** The answer is fairly certain in *What is an apple? What is a child? What is an egg?* in *What is beauty? What is knowledge? What is water?* and—note—in *What is the sea?* The question could not be applied to *Shakespeare* in the same way: for a special name we usually expect the question *Who is . . .?* or *Where is,* e.g. *London?** With the other words given in **71,** both *What is . . .?* and *What is a . . . ?* are possible—at least, so I was informed by native-English speakers to whom I applied this test without explaining why I was doing so. Incidentally, my informants voted for *What is breakfast?.*

Articles with Proper Nouns

101. We have already had *the Shakespeare* (**24**); and could have *a Shakespeare,* i.e. a man of that stature; and *Shakespeares* too (**98**). Proper Nouns in Case 6 occur in instances like *the Barretts,* i.e. the family of people named Barrett.

---

* We could, however, say *What was Shakespeare? A poet or a playwright? What is London, a town or a city?*

102. It is understandable that special names should be preceded by *the* when composed of class-words. *The Union of Soviet Socialist Republics* exemplifies **87** (*a*)—it answers the question *Which union? The Peak*, the name of a mountain, is an example of **87** (*c*). *The United States, the British Isles, the Philippine Islands*, etc.—**87** (*a*) in the plural. Columbus, sailing west to discover India, discovered several new Indias instead, and gave us *the Indies*, plural of **87** (*c*).

103. Apart from countries with political boundaries, such as those quoted in **102**, certain geographical features which have to be distinguished one from another also have names beginning with *the*. *The Red Sea* is a specified sea, and so is *the Indian Ocean*. *The Giant Mountains* form a distinctive mountain range. *The River Nile* is that river and no other. The class-word can be omitted when the specifying word is sufficient to identify the feature: *The Mediterranean* (Sea), *the Pacific* (Ocean), *the Sahara* (Desert), *the* (River) *Ganges*. Note the effect of omitting 'islands' and 'mountains': *the Philippine Islands, the Philippines; the Himalaya Mountains, the Himalayas; the Rocky Mountains, the Rockies*. The class-word cannot be omitted when the specifying word by itself is inadequate identification: *the Red, the Indian, the Giants, the British* (as an abbreviation for *the British Isles*) could be applied to too many other things for the meaning to be clear.

104. A signal of specification is not felt to be necessary with names of lakes and individual mountains; thus *Everest, Lake Baikal*.

105. It is important, however, that ships should be distinguished one from another: *Is that the 'Queen Elizabeth' or the 'Queen Mary'?* An account of naval manœuvres in Nelson's day (early 19th century) refers first to *the 'Swift' frigate*, then to *the Swift*.* Railway trains and aeroplanes are now being specified in this way. *The* has long been a signal of specification for *inns, taverns* and *hotels*—*the Crown* (Inn), *the Elephant and Castle* (Tavern),† *the Grand* (Hotel). Names of newspapers and periodicals are also preceded by *the*— *The Times, The Lancet, The Asahi, The Mainichi*—whether as an indication that one must be distinguished from another, or to indicate, for example, the one and only *Times*. *The Bible* (literally 'the book') is a solitary member of its class, as is *the Koran*, or *the Odyssey*, or

---

* Sailors on board the *Swift*, for whom that vessel was home, spoke of it simply as *Swift*. See **113** (*f*).

† In South London, mentioned in Shakespeare's *Twelfth Night*.

the Iliad. But we can borrow a bible, i.e. a copy of *the Bible*, just as we can borrow *a 'Hamlet'* or *a 'War and Peace'*.

106. One way of tracing the tendencies of living grammar is by observing native-speakers in the act of creating their own idiom. I once worked in Crespel Street in Brussels for an organisation that was looking for other premises. We found what we wanted in Avenue Marnix, and referred to it as '*the Marnix building*'. Soon, perhaps in imitation of those whose lead we followed socially, we were calling it *the Marnix*. But our original office remained *Crespel*. Thus, from Crespel, we would say, 'Are these things going over to the Marnix?'; but, speaking from the new building, 'My books are still over at Crespel.' (See **118**.)

107. It may be in such circumstances that English usage has grown up with apparent inconsistency in the use of the articles, as in other respects. With many of the names used in daily life by English-speakers, there is no way, without becoming intimately acquainted with that life, of telling when convention or fashion or accident will decide whether we say *the Marnix building* or *the Marnix* or just *Marnix*. All three are possible in English: one has to know which happens to have been adopted in each case. The student need not worry about the parochial whims of British or American speakers unless he wishes to make a special study of them. But he needs to know in what ways the language can operate on such occasions. In the case of life in London, it operates with the following results:

(*a*) *Buckingham Palace, Hampton Court, St. Paul's Cathedral, Victoria Station* (or simply *Victoria*), *London Bridge, Regent Street, Horseferry Road, Covent Garden* (both market and opera-house), *Marble Arch*. Note that '*the Regent's Park*', named after *the Regent* (**87**, *c*), was popular a century ago, and that *the Marble Arch* is not dead yet.

(*b*) *The Tower of London* (or *the Tower*), *the Monument* (the one commemorating the Great Fire of London in 1666), *the Strand* (a class-word—cf. *the Peak*, quoted in **102**), *the Edgware Road* (the road leading to Edgware), *the Old Vic* (Theatre), *the British Museum, the London Zoo*. But see **113** (*c*).

108. One might rationalise some of these usages by arguing, for example, that with *London University* we are not admitting the need for specification—there is only one university in London and this is it; whereas with *the London Library* we have in mind the existence of other libraries, in London and elsewhere, but this is the one we are

specifying. Similarly, *Edinburgh University* and *the Edinburgh Festival*. However, when the class-word precedes the proper noun, *the* is used in any case: *The Tower of London, the University of London*, etc. *The* being a mark of distinction, *the University of Oxford* is felt to be more ceremonial than *Oxford University*.

Mass-words used as Unit-words

109.   Which abstractions and substances are customarily conceived as units in English is a matter of fact, and the student must observe the facts in good usage. The dictionary will help him here, and so will H. E. Palmer's *Grammar of English Words*. He will find that *Virtue is its own reward*, that *Patience is a virtue* and that *Faith, hope and charity are virtues*; that we speak of *faiths*, but to mean the ideas in which we have faith, and *charities* to mean not 'acts of charity' but organised objects of charity. We speak of *doubts* and *injustices*— but not *justices*, unless we are referring to judges. *Information* and *progress* would only occur in normal English in Cases 1 and 5. So would *advice*, *advices* being regarded as an old-fashioned, stilted equivalent of news. *News*, on the contrary, is plural in form but takes a singular verb, and it, too, occurs only in Cases 1 and 5. *Weather* is generally found only in the same two cases, though we find the expression *in all weathers* (Case 2).

'Classifiers' used with Mass-words

110.   One example of a substance or material is often indicated in English by 'classifiers', rather as in Chinese. The commonest and most useful classifier is *piece*, which can be used with abstractions as well as substances; e.g. *a piece of paper, of cloth, of wood, of bread, of meat, of advice, of information, of news*. No shape is suggested by *piece*, but a piece of a more definite form can be indicated by *slice, strip, grain, stick, lump, heap, ball, sheet, block*, and similar words in constant household use. We can have *a slice of bread, cake or meat; a strip of cloth, of land; a grain of rice, of corn; a stick of chalk, of dynamite; a lump of lead, of coal; a heap of earth, of rubbish; a ball of wool; a sheet of paper, of metal rolled thin; a block of wood, of ice*. Colloquially, we can have *a bit* (i.e. a small piece) *of anything* solid. Some words have their own classifiers: *a loaf of bread, a joint of meat, a rasher of bacon, a clod of earth*. Similarly, we speak of *a blade of grass*; but we can pick out *a* (single) *hair* from the hair which grows on our heads. *Money* is a mass-word; the corresponding unit-word is *coin*, or *note*, or *pound, dollar*, etc. All the classifiers men-

tioned above refer to solids, though we can speak metaphorically of *a sheet of water*, referring to smooth surface. The liquid equivalent of *bit* would be *drop*.

111.   When we do find a word for a substance or abstraction used with *a* it is either to indicate *a kind of* that substance or a finished product consisting of it. *A good wine* is a good *kind* of wine; *a bread* is a *kind* of bread, not a loaf. The same could be said of *an iron, a paper, a cloth*. But also and commonly *an iron* is a household implement; *a paper* is a newspaper, a written report or dissertation, or a set of examination questions; *a cloth* is the finished article spread over a table, or a small piece of cloth for cleaning. Similarly, *a work* is a product of work, a new creation. We speak of *a work of art, the works of Dickens, the devil and all his works*. Ordinary human beings merely *do a job*, or, if they wish to avoid that humble word, *a piece of work*; more pompously they *fulfil a task*. *A play*, too, is a new creation—a story written for acting. A form of play complete in itself would be *a game*.

The Special Case of 'PEOPLE'

112.   With its individualistic conception of society, English envisages *people* only as units. If the question asked in **100** were applied to *people*, we would usually expect it to be *What are* . . .? However, *people* can refer either to two or more persons taken together, or to a racial group. *The people* also means the general public. The complete 'declension' of *person* and *people* would be:

	Two or more persons		Racial group
Case 1 person	—		—
Case 2 persons	people		peoples
Case 3 a person	—		a people
Case 4 persons	people		peoples
Case 5 the person	—		the people
Case 6 the persons	the people		the peoples

People is followed by a plural verb, e.g. *are*, invariably in column two, and generally in column three.

Unit-words Unmarked by *a* or *the*

113.   Instances of unit-words in Case 1 are:
  (*a*) Notices: *Footpath to beach* (*notice* seen at *holiday resort*).

(*b*) Notes: as in *words* italicised in *brackets* in *line* above and in this note.

(*c*) Signs and labels: *Arrow-head, 5th century* (in a museum), *Strand, Edgware Road* (street signs).

(*d*) Newspaper headlines: *Bride-to-be Abducted at Church Gate.* Here, the absence of articles, besides saving space, tempts the reader to look for the specific details provided in the article below the head-line.

(*e*) Telegrams: WIRE DATE CONTRACT SIGNED LETTER FOLLOWS The receiver of this telegram should know which contract and which date were meant; in any case, the 'letter' that 'follows' would supply the necessary specification.

(*f*) Certain words in constant, communal use, when specification is no longer felt by the community concerned to be necessary: *School begins next Monday. Term ends on December 19th* (spoken as 'December the nineteenth'). *To dine in Hall* (the dining-hall of a college at Oxford or Cambridge). In a British colony, the Government is usually referred to as '*Government*', just as the British people speak of their parliament as '*Parliament*'. See also the footnote to paragraph **105**, on '*Swift*'.

(*g*) Names of relationships used as Proper Nouns: *Father* (nominative case) *says we mustn't. Give it to Mother* (objective case). *Thank you, Uncle* (vocative case). *Baby, Nurse* and *Sister* (meaning 'senior nurse') can also be used in this way, in all three cases. Names of certain ranks and titles are used likewise, though now usually in the vocative case only: *Yes, Colonel. Carry on, Sergeant. I'm feeling much better, Doctor. That's all I know, Inspector* (of police); similarly, *Officer* and *Constable* in the police-force. Such words refer to people who hold a respected position in the family or community; but this kind of usage would not apply to persons of rank high above the level of the ordinary man. One would therefore speak of *the King, the Duke, the President* (in accordance with **89**), but not say *I'm happy to meet you, Duke.* Here, British English would use a form of address like *Your Grace* (for a Duke or Archbishop) or *Sir* (which could be used very widely as a sign or respect, in addressing the head of the state or an ordinary stranger).

(*h*) Names of definite appointments. Note: *He is a bank manager*— he is a member of that class. But he is *Manager of the Westminster Bank.* Similarly, *He is President of the Republic, Rector of the University, Director of the Department.* In these last four examples, *the Manager, the President,* etc., are also possible and in fact add a tone of distinction to the title (cf. **89** and **108**). Observe the difference between *He was (the) Minister of Finance* (of that particular country, at that particular date), and *He was a Minister of Finance* (one of a series of Ministers of Finance).

(*i*) in certain types of expression where words are put in couples or in a list: *They became man and wife* (were married). *People worked day and night, in office, field and factory.*

(*j*) with a noun 'in apposition' to another: *Thomas Hardy, author of 'Tess of the d'Urbervilles'*. Omission of *the* in this case is not obligatory.

114.   There are many fixed expressions composed of preposition + noun (e.g. *in fact*) or verb + noun (*give way*) in which we are not concerned with a specific example of the concept represented by the noun. Other examples: *in doubt, at ease, in general, at rest, in time, at war, at work; do harm, make peace, make progress.* The instances just quoted are of abstractions and it is understandable that they should occur in Case 1. But unit-words can also fit into this pattern when we are concerned not with a particular example of the concept but with, for example,

(*a*) an action communally associated with the object referred to; *go to bed* (to rest), *be* (*or stay*) *in bed, get out of bed; go to church* (to pray, to attend a service); *go to hospital, be* (*or stay*) *in hospital* (for treatment); *go to market* (to buy or sell); *be at office** (working), *go to office** (to work), *be in office* (hold an appointment); *go to prison* (as a punishment); *go to school* (to study or teach).

(*b*) with the class of object, rather than any particular example of it, by which something is conveyed: *to go by bus, by car, by coach, on foot, by plane, by sea, by train;* to send a letter *by hand, by special messenger.*

(*c*) with the idea in general, or the thing in the abstract: *at dawn, on edge, in goal, in hand, at night, in person, in question, on record, in reply, at sea.*

115.   Such word-groups tend to form when they express a fixed idea that constantly occurs in a community and when it is not felt necessary to specify the object represented by the noun. When one of those nouns is used to refer to a specific object or to express a different idea, then the fixed expression is no longer operative. Thus: *the postman goes to the hospital to deliver letters.* He does not in this case go for treatment; and he goes to a hospital specified by the context in which that statement is made. In *His story is on record* we do

---

* This usage may not have become generally established, but it is common enough in London, where office-going is an important communal activity (see **113,** *f* and **115**).

not say *where*, but in *Everything he told us is on the record* we refer to the known record of a particular incident. Note the difference between *by sea* (**114,** *b*) and *by the sea*, i.e. *beside the sea* (**91**).

116. Specification is sometimes accompanied by a change of preposition, notably from *at* (unmarked, unspecified dimension) to *on* or *in*, where dimension is more clearly indicated (see Chapter Eleven), e.g. *at sea*, but *on the sea* (on the surface) and *in the sea* (in the water); *at night*, but *in, or during, the night* (a specific night, or *the night* as distinct from *the day*).

117. It should be noted that the kind of expressions dealt with in **114** must be accepted by the community; that in some situations they are optional (one can say *in spring, summer, autumn, winter* or *in the spring*, etc., *go to university* or *go to the university*); while in some situations they have not found acceptance at all (e.g. we say *in bed* but not *on bed,† *in chair, or *on chair). On the other hand, in some situations a different pattern has become established: e.g. *go to the theatre to see a play* or *to the station to catch a train*; *in the morning, in the afternoon, in the evening*. In these last examples we find the tendency noted in **91** of marking off known points on the map, either in space (*the theatre/the cinema/the bank*) or in time (*the afternoon/the evening*; *the summer/the winter*).

Man *v* the Animals

118. Why *man* but *the animals*? '*Home* is where one starts from' (Eliot, 'East Coker'). We say, 'This is *home*. We're *at home*. Go out, and come *home* again.' There is no need to specify which home, or this part of the map as distinct from another. That kind of specification only begins when we venture away from our point of primary concern. But when the point of primary concern becomes the school, as it does with educationists, they can properly ask, 'Should moral education be given *at school* or *in the home*? (Note the change of preposition, as in **116**.) *Crespel* (**106**) was 'home'; *the Marnix*, a definite sector of the outside world. Londoners live *in town*, but like to spend their holidays *in the country* or *by the sea*. English-speaking people in Greece go from *Athens*, centre of *Attica*, down to *the Peloponnese*. In Japan, they go from *Tokyo* down to *the Kansai*. It is perhaps typical of man, at least of the English-speaking man, and now of woman, that he, and she, should regard themselves as such a

---

† The asterisk *before* an expression means that the expression is unacceptable.

centre, surveying the rest of creation, *the child*,† *the animals* (i.e. the different classes of animals), *the birds* and *the plants*.

What constitutes specification?

119. *German is a language* or *David Jones is a doctor* does not tell us which language is German or which of a row of strange doctors is David Jones. They only tell us to what classes of things German and David Jones belong.

The Influence of Adjectives

120. Nor, in the examples in **119,** are *language* and *doctor* made identifiable by a merely descriptive adjective, e.g. *difficult* or *good*. An adjective inserted into the patterns *no article + noun, a + noun, the + noun*, does not necessarily affect the use of the article at all. Thus, with an adjective, *this is 'water* becomes *this is 'hot water; the Nile is a 'river* becomes *the Nile is a 'wide river; Canberra is the 'capital of 'Australia* becomes *Canberra is the 'new 'capital*, etc. (for stress in *the new capital*, see **90,** *c*).

121. The only difference an adjective can make is to turn the pattern *a + noun* into *the + noun*, **when the adjective unquestionably identifies the object or sample represented by the noun.** If, for example, I have six cups, all of different sizes, and one of them broken, specification (if we wish to make it) is assured by the adjectives in *the 'broken cup, the 'smallest one, the 'biggest*. Adjectives like *first, next, last, same*, and superlatives like *best, most interesting*, are therefore usually preceded by *the*. But not invariably: one can win *a first prize* if more than one first prize is awarded or if there are several competitions; and similarly *a last word, a best-seller, a most* (i.e. very) *interesting subject*. Note also: *Rome had an empire, called the Roman Empire. Chinese is a difficult language—the Chinese language is perhaps the most difficult of all.*

122. A mistake frequently made by foreign students of English is on the pattern *I am studying *the Roman law*. We study *law*, and, in accordance with **120,** *Roman law*, regarding the latter as a kind or example of law, not as an identified unit or sample. *The Roman law* would refer to a specific piece of legislation—Law No. so-and-so—

† Or *children* (Case 2). Educationists speak of *the child* as an imaginary representative of that class: cf. *the student*, **92.**

and it assumes that the hearer or reader knows which one is meant. *The Roman law* could also, however, refer to the whole body of Roman legislation,* as distinct from some other body of legislation, if we wish to make that distinction deliberately: thus, *Greek law maintained such-and-such,* but *the Roman law held the opposite view.* This is a stylistic usage and a student should not attempt it if *Roman law* is what he really means.

123. Notice how the addition of an adjective does not alter the original pattern of *no article + noun*.

(*a*) *Mass-words in Case 1:*

I am studying	architecture	—*modern architecture*
	art	—*classical art*
	economics	—*nineteenth century economics*
	history	—*ancient history*
	language (the phenomenon)	—*French language*
	literature	—*English literature*
	music	—*German music*
	painting	—*Italian painting*

He imports	coal	—*brown coal*
	glass	—*Venetian glass*
	paper	—*Japanese paper*
	wine	—*Spanish wine*

(*b*) *Unit-words in Case 2:*

He imports	bicycles	—*English bicycles*
	cameras	—*German cameras*
	cars	—*American cars*

124. Note the difference between *Russian people* (Case 2, or Case 4) and *the Russian people* (Case 6), the former meaning 'Russian people in general' or 'more than one Russian', the latter specifying one group of people as distinct from another.

125. Note *Spanish 'wine, Japanese 'paper* (Case 1: stress on 'wine', 'paper'; meaning a kind of wine, of paper); but *the 'wine trade, the*

---

* Cf. *law*, the concept in general, and *the law*, the whole corpus of legislation, as in *We must respect the law.*

'*paper industry* (stress still on 'wine', 'paper'), where the stressed words specify a separate trade or industry.

126.   As we saw in **85,** a name in the possessive form ('s) coming before a noun is felt to be sufficient in itself to identify the object (*Napoleon's hat*). But a name unmarked by *'s* and serving as an adjunct can be preceded by *the*. Compare *Shakespeare's theatre* with *the Shakespeare theatre*, i.e. the theatre devoted to performances of Shakespeare's works. Incidentally, *the 'Shakespeare 'theatre*, as the phrase is generally used, is an example of **87** (*c*), and stress falls more or less equally on both adjunct and noun. Yet it could be used as an example of **87** (*a*), with stress on the first noun, e.g. *I mean the 'Shakespeare theatre, not the 'Old 'Vic.*

The Influence of Restricting Phrases and Clauses

127.   Note the difference between (*a*) *Fruit in this country is plentiful*, and (*b*) *The fruit in this country is delicious*. In (*a*), *in this country* tells us where fruit is plentiful; in (*b*) the same phrase tells us which part of the whole field of fruit is delicious (**94**). Example (*b*) could also refer to *the fruit* as distinct from some other class of thing (**87,** *b*), e.g. *the vegetables*.

128.   Phrases beginning with *of* frequently identify the object, though not invariably. We feel that *Roman law* indicates a kind of law, while *the law of Rome* marks out a definite sector in the field of law, distinct from other sectors. Compare the examples in **123** with *the architecture of the present day, the economics of the nineteenth century, the history of China, the wine of the country*, etc.

129.   In phrases beginning with *of*, the student must be careful to distinguish between form and meaning: it is not merely that the word *of* attracts the word *the*, but that a phrase beginning with *of* frequently serves to specify an example of the concept or to mark out a definite sector of the field. Compare, therefore, *the Peace of Versailles* (specific example) with *peace of mind* (i.e. peace in, or in respect of, the mind); *the freedom of university life* (as distinct from the restrictions of life in school, office or factory) with *freedom of speech* (i.e. freedom to speak one's mind); *the love of God* (i.e. God's love) with *love of God* (felt towards God). We have specific examples of the concept in *I look forward to the pleasure of accompanying you, the honour of taking the Chair at your lecture, the satisfaction of knowing that everything is settled.*

130. Relative clauses are a common means of specification: *Life can be hard, but nothing could be more agreeable than the life we are leading at the moment.* But again, be careful: make sure that the relative clause really identifies the object or sample. Compare *the work which has accumulated while I've been away* (that definite part of the field of work) with *Work, which is the lot of every man, takes up most of our waking hours:* here the relative clause is making a comment on work in general.

Fixed Expressions and Freedom of Choice

131. See **46**. As we have seen in this chapter, the articles are subject to many conventional usages. In *go to church* and *go to the theatre* we can trace two understandable tendencies (**114, a**, and **91**), but we must accept the fact that one tendency has been followed with *church*, another with *theatre*. In the same way, we must accept *at first, at last* side by side with *at the beginning, at the end, at the centre, in the middle*, and a great number of other expressions which have become stereotyped, with restricted meanings.

132. Apart from fixed expressions, certain usage is rendered inescapable by the context. In *Work, which is the lot of every man*, the context requires *work* to be in Case 1: nothing else would make sense. On other occasions, one finds an apparently 'free variant': *in summer* and *in the summer* are both acceptable, and we can use one or the other with no apparent distinction of meaning. Nevertheless, a good writer might say (*in*) *the summer*, as distinct from (*in*) *the winter*, or (*in*) *summer* when no such distinction is relevant.

133. There remains in speech, and even more in writing, wide scope for free use of the articles, so long as one does not break the conventions referred to in **131** and so long as one makes a socially-accepted correlation between meaning and form. Thus while **The work, which is the lot of every man* is impossible, *I must attend to the work that has accumulated since I've been away* is 'right' if one wishes to draw attention to specific tasks, and *I must attend to work that has accumulated*, etc., is also 'right' if *work* is conceived as a vague mass, or if the emphasis falls elsewhere in the sentence. In other words, though *work* in the last example is *formally* restricted by the relative clause, and is restricted in meaning too, the fact that it is so is irrelevant to the speaker who makes that statement clear-mindedly. It is the intuitive or conscious awareness of such subtleties that helps to give good writing precision.

69

CHAPTER SEVEN

The Tenses

134.   In the tenses we are concerned with aspects of ACTIVITY and aspects of TIME. Time itself might be regarded as an aspect of activity, in so far as the idea of it arises out of the thought of events fulfilled or foreseen, and it is only in terms of events that it can be measured. I consider *being* to be a form of activity.

Activity

135.   Activity is an important element in the experience of native-English speakers, who see it from several different points of view. To understand its expression in the English tense-system, we must imagine—

(*a*) The general idea of an act, not containing any of the distinctions referred to in (*b*) to (*f*).

(*b*) The act seen as a completed whole, synoptically: this could be called the strong form of the unmarked member (see **38**), and in expression it is identical with (*a*).

(*c*) The act uncompleted, imagined as action in progress, the process rather than the accomplishment; the act seen analytically. (*b*) : (*c*) :: *all* : *some*.

(*d*) The act performed once.

(*e*) The act performed repeatedly; a whole series of acts; the series viewed synoptically.

(*f*) A partial or uncompleted series of acts. (*b*) : (*c*) :: (*e*) : (*f*).

136.   Other aspects of activity, expressed other than by changes in verb-form, will be discussed in Chapter Eight.

137.   This subject, like the articles, could be illustrated very well by animated pictures or diagrams. On paper, we might show

(*a*), in **135**, as a vague mass, representing the general concept (cf. Case 1 of the articles, **97**);

(b), like this:

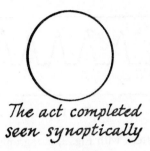

The act completed
seen synoptically

FIG. 12

(c), like this:

FIG. 13

(action in progress: the thin line represents TIME,
the thick line represents ACTION)

or like this:

FIG. 14

(the uncompleted act)

(d), by a single reaction of an electric needle, thus:

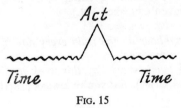

FIG. 15

71

(*e*), by a complete series of reactions, seen synoptically:

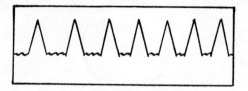

FIG. 16

(Compare this pattern with Fig. 3, paragraph **53**—*Every*.)

(*f*), by part of such a series, or a series proceeding indefinitely, thus:

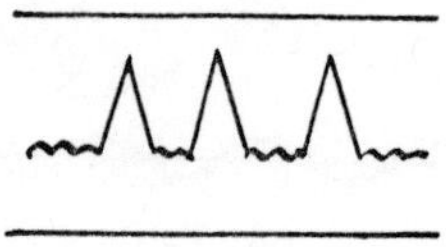

FIG. 17 (i)

or

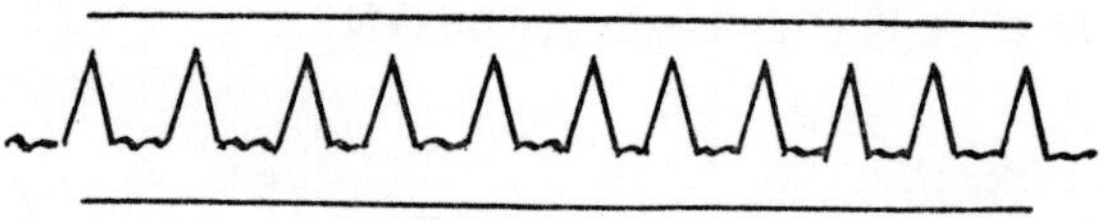

FIG. 17 (ii)

(Compare Fig. 17 (i) with Fig. 7, Paragraph **57**—*Some*)

138.   Examples:

(*a*) *God* **works** *in a mysterious way.*

(*b*) *I* **tell** *you it's true.* (I tell you, definitely, now. Note: I have not said, 'I'm telling you'.)

(*c*) *Listen carefully to what* **I'm telling** *you.* (Listen while the telling is in process; I haven't finished yet.)

(*d*) *I* **see** *a ship—can you see it?*

(*e*) *I* **see** *my neighbour on the train every day but we never speak except to say 'Good morning'.*

(*f*) **I'm playing** *tennis every day this week to get practice for the tournament* (partial series). *But* **you're always practising** (series going on indefinitely).

72

139.　These aspects of activity are reflected in English in the following scheme:

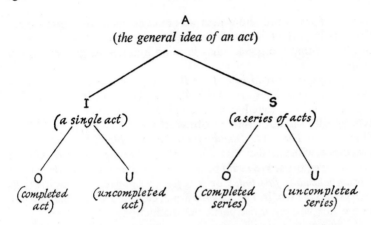

140.　Take *I go* as an example:

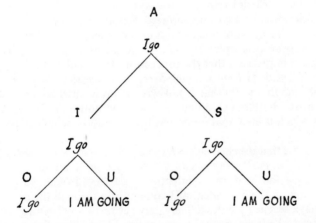

141.　**A** is the weak unmarked form; **O** is the strong unmarked form; and **U** the marked form. Remember that the marked form is the one we use when we wish to make some special distinction. In choosing **U** we ought to have in mind the kind of emphasis explained and exemplified in **135** and **137,** (*c*) and (*f*). Note that **A, I, S, I O** and **S O** are expressed by the same unmarked form (*I go*); and that **I U** and **S U** are expressed by the same marked form (*I am going*). In other words, **we say** *I go* **until and unless we are concerned with the uncompleted aspect of the act or series.**

142.   I repeat 'until and unless we are concerned with' that aspect. What is important is not so much the objective fact as the *aspect* of the fact that the speaker has in mind and wishes to express. For example:

(*a*) In saying *I read in bed for half an hour before I turn out the light*, I refer to a series (of acts) which happens to be incomplete; but it is not that fact that I wish to emphasise. I am viewing the series synoptically without wishing to draw attention to the idea of **137** (*f*). Similarly, in *The River Danube flows into the Black Sea*, we are not concerned with the fact that the Danube is in *process* of flowing or that it *never stops*. We *could* be so concerned and say *The Danube is flowing unusually fast today* or *It is for ever flowing and emptying its waters into the sea*. In *The Danube flows*, etc., we see the phenomenon as a whole without those particular distinctions.

(*b*) In saying *I'm telling you*, I am obviously concerned with the process of telling and with the incompletion of it. My telling may (or may not) be accomplished. If it is, that is irrelevant and is not the aspect to which I want to draw your attention.

(*c*) In reporting two uncompleted actions, we may wish to emphasise the progress of one but not of the other; e.g. *As I stand here, the procession is entering the hall*. It would be vain of me, besides giving the impression that the procession was small and its entrance hasty, if I said *As I am standing here, the procession enters the hall*, though grammatically that is not wrong. Both verbs could take the **O** form and both the **U** in that sentence. But notice the first example given, which is an actual quotation from a radio commentary.

143.   Note that *the uncompleted act may eventually be finished, or not.* In saying *I'm putting my pen on the desk*, i.e. in describing an action in progress (not stating my intention—see **153**), I ought to be concentrating on the movement of hand and pen through the air before they have reached the desk. They may get there, or they may not. It happens to be in my power to stop them. **I U** can therefore be easily applied to a *voluntary* act.

144.   The now popular doctrine that the difference between *I am going* and *I go* is that the former expresses the act performed at the time of speaking, the latter the act performed habitually, is due to the high frequency of examples of **I U** and **S O** in ordinary speech and to a rough generalisation drawn from a comparison of these two parts

of the scheme outlined in **140**. One could reach the opposite conclusion by comparing examples of **I O** (act performed at this moment) and **S U** (habitually—see example in **29**). Admittedly, there are many examples of **I U** in which the predominant idea is one of 'activity at the time of speaking', e.g. (*I can't understand you*)—*are you trying to speak English?* Examples of this kind could be compared with ones in which the predominant idea is that of the act performed *habitually*, e.g. *Do you speak English at home?* In these examples, the change of verb-form makes it clear that in *are you trying* I mean *at this moment*, while in *do you speak* I mean *usually*. But in linking *are you trying* with *at this moment*, and *do you speak* with *usually* and generalising accordingly, we are reasoning from only part of the evidence. It is quite possible to say, as I do now, *I stop work at this moment—I'm usually feeling pretty tired by this hour of night.* In any case, in *are you trying*, as in *I'm usually feeling* and generally in the verb-forms in *-ing*, there is the sense of incompletion which is the essential marking.

145. The difference between momentary action and habitual activity is therefore not expressed in English by a change of verb-form, except incidentally in certain types of usage. As the diagram in **140** shows, **I** and **S** are identical in form. The difference is contained in the context, though it is underlined by adverbial expressions such as *at this moment* or *regularly, often, sometimes, always. Now* is not a good example of such an adverb since it can be used for regular activity as well as momentary action, completed as well as uncompleted, e.g. *Now I put down my pen* (**I O**), *Now I am looking out of the window* (**I U**), *Now I write all my letters myself*—(*I used to dictate them*) (**S O**), *Now I am writing twenty pages a day*—(*last year I could only do six*) (**S U**). It can also be used with both Past and Future Tenses: *I saw him just now. Now we'll stop.*

Physical Movement and Mental Perception

146. Just as some of the things we talk about can be conceived more easily in the mass than as units, and *vice versa* (Chapter Five, **98** ff.), so some of our actions are more easily imagined as completed acts than as uncompleted processes. The commentator on the football match, **28**) saw the game as a series of accomplished acts; e.g. *Johnson passes to Roberts, Roberts to Watkins, Watkins takes it forward, oh he slips past the centre half beautifully, he shoots*—all perfect examples of **I O**. Watching a boat race, the commentator is, by the nature of the event, more conscious of movement in progress; e.g.

Oxford are rowing splendidly—one—two—three—four—they're just coming in sight of Hammersmith Bridge. Ah—Cambridge are increasing ing their pace—all **I U**. Here the reader must again be warned against generalising from incidental factors. The movements of football may be *quicker*, those of rowing may *take longer*; but the essential factors determining the usage of the verb-form is not speed, or length of duration, but rather the fact that the speed makes the spectator more aware of the completed act, the duration more aware of the action in progress.

147.   By their nature, acts like *walk, run, read, write, work, play*, are more likely to be expressed by **I U** and **S O** than by **I O**. They can be expressed by **I O** none the less, and are so, more often than we sometimes suppose (see **26–28**).

148.   On the other hand, it is difficult (though for a scientist certainly not impossible) to catch oneself or someone else in the middle of a single act of *seeing* or *hearing*. *To see* or *to hear* is to receive a sensory impression through the appropriate organ. The reception of the impression is an involuntary act: this is relevant in so far as we cannot normally prevent the completion of the act. Thus, as we commonly say in English, *you see*—or *you don't* (*see*), *you can't help yourself.* Yet sometimes it is possible for us to perceive the reception of a visual image in an unfinished state. Wearing the wrong spectacles or having dined not wisely but too well, *I might be seeing double.* Such occurrences of *see* in **I U** may be rare, but they help to explain why *see* is normally found only in the completed aspect. Yet in **S U** *see* would occur as frequently as any other verb, since we have no difficulty in imagining an uncompleted series of the acts of reception; e.g. *Mary is seeing that young man too often.**

149.   In contrast with *seeing*, the voluntary act of *looking* (*at something*) is easy to imagine in **I U**. *See* : *look at* : : *take a snapshot* : *focus the camera*. Note that I can go on focusing for a long time, achieving my object or not. *Duration* is thus a factor in **U**; but again the essential factor is not the length of the duration but *emphasis* on the duration and on the incompletion of the process. It is possible for **O** to last longer than **U**.

---

* The argument that *see* in this case does not really mean *see* but means something else does not alter the fact that *is seeing* is possible in English. In any case, this argument should not be used to justify the 'rule' that *see* cannot occur in the continuous tenses. What else could *see* mean in *I'm seeing too many pictures—I can't look at any more?*

150. Parallel with *see v look* (*at*) is *hear v listen* (*to*). *Smell, taste* and *feel* express both involuntary and voluntary action, and correspond with both *see* and *look at* accordingly. Other words which occur more easily in **I O** than in **I U** are *know, remember, forget, want, like, love, think, believe, doubt, hope, wish, suppose,* and similar expressions of perception and feeling. *You know it, remember it, like it, want it, believe it—or you don't.* Here the teacher must distinguish between helpful advice and absolute statement. He would be justified in advising his pupils not to use *know, remember,* etc., in the *-ing* form of the verb, until they are more advanced. He would be wrong in obliging them to learn the 'rule' that these words are not used in the Present Continuous Tense at all. Just as all nouns in English can, potentially, fill all six Cases (**98**), so all verbs (except the so-called auxiliaries and anomalous finites*) can potentially fill all the positions in **140**.

151. The difficulty of fitting into **I U** is not a peculiarity of verbs of perception and feeling. It may apply to any act that cannot by its nature be seen analytically. I can analyse the act of walking to the door, comment on it as I go along, and stop in the middle of it. I can hardly do that with opening the door, switching on one electric light, or shutting my book, without the help of a slow-motion camera. *I am opening the door, switching on the light, shutting my book* are therefore misleading as examples of the Present Continuous Tense. *The caretaker is* (*going round*) *opening the doors and switching on the lights* would be a better illustration of the meaning of this tense-form.

Psychological Subtleties

152. Since we are concerned with the connection between grammatical form and what we have in mind, the whole aspect of grammar we are discussing in this book is more or less psychological; and it is not surprising that it abounds with psychological subtleties. The student may be familiar with the difference between *I think you're right* (I have formed that opinion, or come to that conclusion) and *Be quiet, I'm thinking* (giving thought to a problem: cf. *looking, listening*). He may be puzzled to hear *I'm thinking you're right*: this is perfectly 'correct' if the speaker is using the marked form to indicate that he is moving towards that conclusion but has not

* *will, shall, would, should, can, could, may, might, must, ought* are not subject to the distinction **O v** U. However, *be, have, do* and *need* are subject to it when used as 'full' verbs and not as auxiliary or modal verbs (except for *being,* passive: **194**); e.g. *Stop making that noise—you're being very tiresome. Mary is having her lesson. I'm doing my homework, and we're all needing to be quiet.*

reached it yet. Thus *I think you're right* is more definite and more committal (besides being safer for the student to imitate) than *I'm thinking you're right*. Similarly, *I'm liking my work*, instead of the more decided and normal *I like it*, suggests that the process of becoming adjusted to it is still going on; or with some speakers, or to some hearers, it might mean I am lingering over its delights. *What are you wanting now?* suggests that you have not made up your mind, that you are in a perpetual state of wanting, or something of that kind. These *nuances* have private meanings and endless possibilities. They are the sort of subtlety into which native-speakers like to take refuge, in social self-defence. Yet the basic distinction between completion and incompletion remains in them.

I am leaving tomorrow

153.   One such subtlety that has become stereotyped and commonly adopted is the use of the uncompleted aspect to indicate action which is about to begin or is due to take place in the future. Thus *we're starting* can mean either that action has begun and is in progress, or that action is about to begin or has been planned, that the required impetus has been given, so that the process has in a sense begun already. Note *I am leaving the country tomorrow and will be abroad for six weeks*. This example provides a contrast between (*am*) (*leav*)*ing* and the future form, *will + infinitive*, and we must discuss this later, both as an aspect of time (**180**) and as a question of mood (**223**). It illustrates an aspect of activity in so far as it suggests and emphasises the idea that I have, or someone else has, decided or arranged that I shall leave the country, and *the process has in that sense begun, though I do not see it yet as completed*—in fact, it may not *be* completed. Note that the terse, businesslike speaker might see the act as completed, and announce firmly *I fly to New York tomorrow*; or, like Julius Caesar, *Tomorrow I cross the Rubicon*. The **O** form can also be used when the speaker's plans are determined for him: *According to schedule I leave at seven in the morning.*

154.   As we are seldom so confident that the future will be fulfilled, the **U** form is commoner than the **O** form in this usage. Yet either may occur in the same situation. Referring to future time, one can say *The ship sails at three* (**I O**) or *The ship is sailing at three* (**I U**). Nor is it true to say that this usage is restricted to verbs indicating movement from one place to another. It occurs frequently as an indication of a planned movement, but it can be applied to any action, e.g. *We're discussing your case on Friday* (that item is on the

agenda of our meeting). However, we could not say *I'm sneezing in a moment or *It's raining tomorrow, since sneezing and raining are not subject to human planning. Moreover, I'm knowing the result tomorrow would be rare, such an act of perception being difficult to imagine in an uncompleted state (150). Nevertheless, we can say I'm seeing the doctor on Tuesday (i.e. I have made an appointment and the process has therefore begun); and with acts of perception the O form is possible, provided such acts are subject to plan, e.g. We hear the results tomorrow (that is when they are due to be published).

155.   We frequently find the pattern (I am) going to (leave) (tomorrow), especially in colloquial English. If the essential factor in the (I am leav)ing pattern is the idea that a process has started in the sense that some event has been planned, the essential factor in the (I am) going to (leave) pattern is a focus on some present activity which the speaker feels certain will lead to some future event. The 'present activity' can be decision, intention or preparation, or it can be an obvious symptom of what the future will bring. The (I am) going to (leave) pattern allows the speaker to state separately the preparation for the event and its accomplishment. (Here note how accomplishment is expressed by the infinitive, to leave, and cf. 277.) The accomplishment, of course, is imagined, not actual, and may not result. Examples:

(a) I am going to end this chapter soon. (This suggests personal decision as well as certainty, so I am ending is also possible here.)

(b) You're going to break that chair if you're not careful. (The speaker sees signs of what will happen and is sure of the result. You do not intend to break the chair, and no one has arranged that you will do so: You're breaking would therefore be wrong in this context.)

(c) I'm going to sneeze in a moment. (The signs are clear—I know what will happen.)

(d) It's going to rain this evening. (Comment as above.)

(e) We're going to understand this eventually.

It will be seen from examples (b), (c), (d) and (e) that the (I am) going to (leave) pattern can be used when the (I am leav)ing pattern cannot. This may explain the very frequent use in conversation of the former, which is often chosen mechanically when the latter would be equally acceptable. The question of am leaving/am going to leave v future will be discussed under Aspects of Time, 179. Meanwhile, am leaving (tomorrow) v am going to leave could be expressed as process imagined as begun in the sense that preliminary decisions, plans or arrangements have been made, v present activity, e.g. personal intentions or objective symptoms, imagined as leading to a completed act.

Time

156. **I O, I U, S O** and **S U** can be combined with **NINE** aspects of time, and the resultant combinations are expressed in the various tense-forms. Aspects of time depend on the speaker's point of primary concern in the natural order of events, and on the direction of his vision from the standpoint he adopts.

157. We might illustrate the natural order of events by a row of numbers, as on the score-board for the game of billiards:

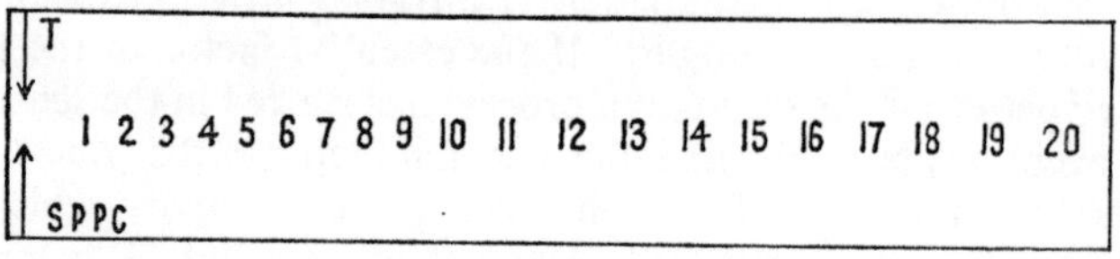

FIG. 18

The arrows on the scoreboard move horizontally and mark the scores of the two players or teams. Let us suppose that the numbers represent happenings, that the top arrow is Time (**T**) and the bottom the speaker's point of primary concern (**S P P C**). **T** moves regularly forward, as if by clock-work. **S P P C** may keep pace with it, be behind it, or in front of it. **T** remains pointing vertically downwards. **S P P C** can swing like the needle of an electrical instrument, so as to point backwards or forwards, at any angle, from whatever position it occupies.

(1) The Weak, Unmarked Aspect

158. In the **FIRST** aspect of time, the 'game' has not begun, and neither of the arrows is 'in play'. **Time, here, is undivided,** or it does not matter; or we are contemplating timelessness. Examples:

The sea breaks eternally on to the shore. (**O**)
The earth **is** *constantly* **revolving** *on its axis.* (**U**)

Breaks and *is revolving* are in the Present Tense. '*All time is eternally present*' (said T. S. Eliot, in 'Burnt Norton'): we regard all time as present until we feel the need to mark some of it off as past or yet to come.

(2) The Strong Unmarked Aspect, i.e. Present Time

159. The **SECOND** aspect is **present time** as distinct from past or future. Here the arrows have moved into play and the scores are equal:

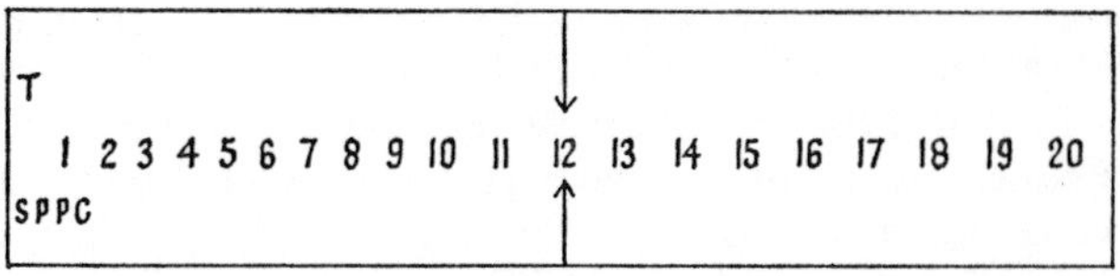

T
1 2 3 4 5 6 7 8 9 10 11 12 13 14 15 16 17 18 19 20
SPPC

FIG. 19

The speaker's attention is focused on an action performed at the time when he is commenting on it. Examples:

(I) *Act completed or action in progress at the* **point NOW.**

(I O) (*a*) **I write** the letter 'e'.
(I U) (*b*) *What* **am I doing? I'm writing.**
(*Note by Author: I am referring to my own actions at this moment.*)

But **S P P C** can also swing backwards and forwards so as to cover a range of activity and events both before and after **T.** The speaker is then considering something that has actually happened as well as something that he imagines will take place. Thus:

(II) *Act completed or action in progress during the* **period NOW.**

(I O) (*c*) **My sister lives** *in England.*
(S O) (*d*) **I** *usually* **get up** *at seven.*
(I U) (*e*) **I am learning** *Arabic*; and
(S U) (*f*) **I'm getting** *up at six this week to revise for an examination.*

S P P C can swing so far backwards and forwards that it covers an unlimited range, which is what we have in **158.** But the range we are concerned with in **159** is limited, though not necessarily defined: it is NOW as distinct from THEN (past) and THEN (future).

160. The previous paragraph could be summarised in this way:

T
Point NOW
The Past
The Future
Period
NOW
Point NOW
SPPC

FIG. 20

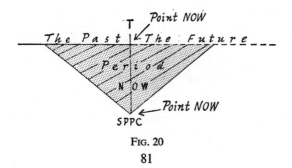

The horizontal line corresponds with the row of numbers in Fig. 19; the vertical line with the line made by the two arrows. The shaded part of Fig. 20 is the *present aspect*. The limits of the period NOW can be close together or far apart. They can be so close together as to meet at the *point* NOW, *the momentary present*, which is synchronous with both **T** and **S P P C**. Or they can extend on either side of the line **T—S P P C** so that the period NOW overlaps with both past and future. Thus, while the events in examples (*a*) and (*b*) of paragraph **159** take place at the point NOW, those in (*c*), (*d*), (*e*), and (*f*) are past and future as well as momentarily present. Incidentally, Fig. 20 will explain why it is possible to say *I saw him just now* and *Now I'll see him.*

Marked Aspects of Time: (3) The Pre-present

161. The THIRD aspect is the **pre-present**, i.e. prelude to the momentary present. Here, **S P P C** is still at the same point as **T**; but whereas the **T** arrow remains pointing vertically downwards, the **S P P C** arrow points back to, and ranges over, the past. In other words, the speaker is concerned with a period of time before and ending at point NOW. (He is not concerned with a specific point of time before NOW, nor with a period ending before NOW. If he were, **S P P C** would be behind T, not level with it.) The pre-present may begin anywhere in the past, no matter how long ago. The beginning of it may or may not be mentioned. The essential factor is that it extends up to and ends at **S P P C**, which is at point NOW. Movement away from the starting point of the pre-present period is expressed by SINCE. However, the speaker has a natural tendency to give more attention to that part of the period which is nearest his viewpoint. Thus the pre-present is frequently the recent past, and hence the dark shading in Fig. 21.

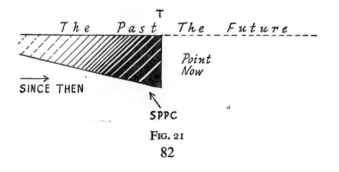

FIG. 21

82

162.   We can move the **S P P C** arrow in different ways. *Either* it can point towards some unspecified moment in the past, or to a number of such moments, or it can move continuously from one moment to a later one and then stop: in all these cases we are concerned with *activity performed or occurring at some time in the period BEFORE now. Or* it can move progressively from a backward-pointing position to a completely vertical one, in which case we are concerned with *activity continuing TILL now.* In other words, in the pre-present we are considering

(I) activity performed or occurring IN* or DURING a period SINCE some point of time in the past and ending now; or within a period ending not later than now, i.e. BY now; or

(II) activity starting from some point in the past (SINCE then), continuing up to the present moment, i.e. TILL (or until) NOW, and lasting FOR such and such a period.

Note the use of YET when the fulfilment of activity in the pre-present is negatived or questioned.

163. Examples:

(I) *Activity BEFORE NOW*

(I O)   (*a*)   **I have written** *the letter 'e'* (cf. **159,** *a*).

(*b*)   **Have you** (*ever*) **been** *to Mexico* (*at any time, yet*)*?*

(*c*)   *No,* **I've** *never* **been** *there* (*yet*).

(*d*)   *Yes,* **I've been** *there once* (time unspecified).

(*e*)   *The Manager is away:* **he has gone** *to Mexico. He has probably arrived by now.*

(*f*)   **I have run** *a mile in 5 minutes* (at some unstated time in the past), *but I couldn't do it now.*

(I U)   (*g*)   *What* **have I been doing?** (**159,** *b*). **I've been writing.**

(*h*)   **It has been raining.** (It stopped five minutes ago, but the streets are still wet.)

(S O)   (*i*)   (The door-bell rings but when I go to the door there is nobody there.) **This has happened** *twice in the last five minutes, and twenty times during the day.*

(S U)   (*j*)   *They* **have been building** *houses everywhere.* (No wonder the place looks so different.)

---

* For explanation of prepositions, see Chapter Eleven.

(II) *Activity CONTINUING TILL NOW*

(I O) *(k)* **I have lived** *here* $\left\{ \begin{array}{l} \textit{since January.} \\ \textit{for the last twelve years.} \\ \textit{most of my life.} \end{array} \right.$

(I U) *(l)* **I have been learning** *Arabic* $\left\{ \begin{array}{l} \textit{since March.} \\ \textit{for six months.} \end{array} \right.$

(S O) *(m)* **I have** (*always*) **got up** *at seven.*

(S U) *(n)* **I have been playing** *tennis every day this week.*

Note the emphasis on the last phase of the pre-present in

> *(o)* **I've** *just** **finished** *a page.*

> *(p)* **Have you finished** *yet?* *No,* **I haven't finished** *yet; not yet. Now* **I've finished;** *now* **I have.**

164. *Action completed before now,* especially if it is immediately before now, will generally produce effects that are *noticeable* now; e.g. *I've just had a bath, and now I'm clean.* The result is perhaps particularly important with native-English speakers who expect action to produce results. However, to understand the tense-form which expresses the pre-present, the student **must consider the aspect of time described in 161 and Fig. 21,** and not allow himself to assume that we use that tense-form *because* the result often happens to be noticeable. If he starts from that assumption, he will find himself in difficulties as soon as he discovers *(a)* that the same tense-form can be used when no result is present at all, e.g. *I have read this book but it has left no impression on my mind whatever*; *(b)* that it is used when the noticeable result is contrary to what he would expect, e.g. (Mother to child) *Look at you. You've just had a bath and now you're filthy*; and *(c)* that the expected result can be present but associated with a *different* tense-form, e.g. *Here are the burglar's footsteps—he came into the house through that window.* Faced with these contradictions, the student is tempted to construct an elaborate system of arguments, rules and exceptions in an attempt to cover up the defect in his premises. The idea of *result* is an important element in the English way of thinking, but it should not be considered as the essential factor in the so-called Present Perfect Tense.

165. *UNcompleted action* in the pre-present might *(a)* be interrupted before now, though it takes place in a *period ending now*; or *(b)* continue until now and then cease; or *(c)*, being uncompleted, go on

---

* *just,* with this aspect of time, points to action completed or occurring shortly before now, during a period ending at the point N O W. Cf. **171** *(c).*

and on, through the present and even into the future. Apply Fig. 13 (**137,** *c*) to Fig. 21, and we have

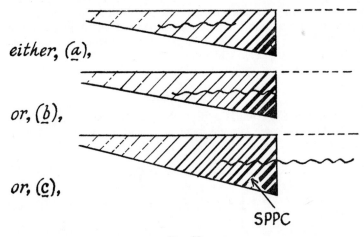

FIG. 22

Examples: (*a*) *Who has been sitting in MY chair* (and has now gone away)? or *It has been raining* (but it stopped five minutes ago); (*b*) *I'll take the wheel now—you've been driving for four hours*; (*c*) *We've been learning English for ten years* (are still, and shall go on, learning it). The continuation of the process after point NOW is therefore something that might occur, and often does. But it need not follow, and often does not. What the speaker is primarily concerned with in this aspect of time is the process, or that part of the process, before *point* NOW, i.e. in the shaded part of Fig. 22.

166.   When the speaker's primary concern is with an act or process begun before point NOW and *continued after it*, he will use *the present aspect* (see Fig. 20). Thus if he wishes to tell us both that he has lived here till now and that he lives here still, he will simply say *This is where I LIVE.* What he cannot do in English is to combine *I live here* (present aspect) with *since* (*a certain date*), which is associated with the *pre-present* (**161**)* and which would have to be used in combination with *I have lived here.*† Likewise, if he wishes to state

---

* Or pre-past. See **177** (*e*) and **306.**

† But note this usage in conversation: *Since when do you paint like that?*—an example of 'double focus'. The reply to that question would have to follow the pattern *I have painted like this since I was a child.*

both that he has been learning English and that he is learning it still, he will simply say *I am learning English* (Fig. 20 again). If he says *I am learning English for six months* (see **163,** *l*) that would mean that the learning process will cease at some future date, either six months from a time in the past when it started, or six months from now. Cf. *I have been staying here for six weeks* (till now) and *I am staying here for six weeks* (till a point of time in the future).

(4) Past Time

167.   For the FOURTH aspect, **the past,** the speaker's primary concern is with *some specific point or period* in the past; in other words, **S P P C** is somewhere behind **T**, like this:

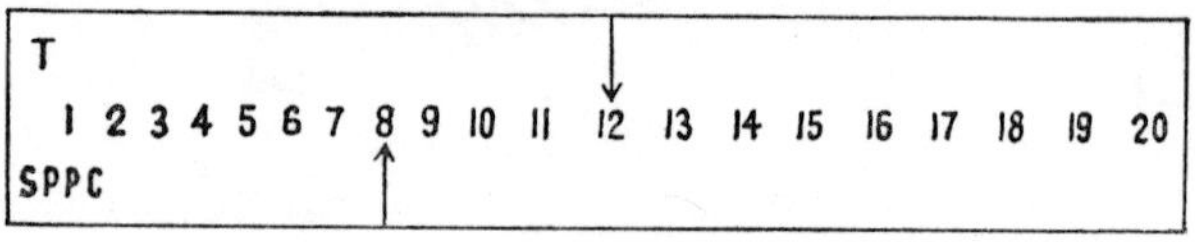

FIG. 23

The distance between **S P P C** and **T** does not matter: it can be great or very small. **S P P C** has now moved from **NOW** to **THEN** (past). The speaker's interest is not directed towards *unspecified time before now* but is concentrated on *a specific time in the past* (cf. the move from unspecifying *a* to specifying *the*: see **93**). This move from unspecified to specified time is often made in English. Examples:

(*a*) Speaker 1. *Have you ever been to Mexico?*
  2. *Yes, twice.*

  1. **Was it** *interesting?*
  2. *Very;* **I enjoyed** *it immensely.*

(*b*)   1. *Pussy cat, pussy cat, where have you been?*
  2. *I've been to London to see the Queen.*

  1. *Pussy cat, pussy cat,* **what did you*** *there?*
  2. **I frightened** *a little mouse under a chair.*

(*Nursery Rhyme*)

In both (*a*) and (*b*) the first speaker shifts his point of view from the momentary present to the time in the past when the action occurred, and speaker 2 follows his example.

* Normal modern English: *what did you do?*

168.   When **S P P C** is in time past, the fact is usually indicated by some adverbial expression of time, e.g. (**I** went *to the National Gallery*) **yesterday, last year, at that time, in 1952, twenty years ago.** Note that A G O marks a time in the past measured back from N O W, a time that becomes **S P P C**. Thus, in Fig. 23, event No. 8 took place four measures of time ago. *Ago* therefore requires the past aspect, just as *since*, in **163,** *k*, requires the pre-present. Note, however, the following type of example, which often confuses students but which should now be quite understandable:

Since $\begin{cases} then, \text{ } (that \text{ } time), \\ the \text{ } time \text{ } (when) \text{ } I \text{ } heard \text{ } her \text{ } sing, \\ \textbf{I heard} \text{ } her \text{ } sing, \end{cases}$ I have always admired her.

169.   Specification of time past can also be made by an adverbial clause (e.g. *when I was a schoolboy*); or by devices other than temporal expressions which help to fix the time the event occurred, e.g. *there*, in **167** (*b*).

170.   The Past Tense, which expresses aspect F O U R, will now be seen as a *signal of specification** of past time—specification being supplied by something (e.g. an adverb) in the context in which that verb-form is used. But the student who really wants to understand what he is doing will not be satisfied with a mechanical association between tense and adverbial expression, e.g. with a mere rote learning of *I went* in conjunction with *a moment ago*. He should be able to appreciate the meaning of the tense without the aid of an adverbial. Consider the following episode from real life. One morning, just before it was time for my family to get up, my wife and I both heard a sound as of footsteps going downstairs. We asked each other, '*What* **was** *that?*', both thinking of the noise we had heard a moment before. A minute later our son Peter appeared at the door of our room with the newspaper. My wife and I spoke simultaneously:

Myself: Oh, it's you. Good, you've brought the paper.
My wife: Oh, it's you. **You went** *down for the paper.*

I used aspect T H R E E, my wife aspect F O U R. Both were 'right' in the circumstances. But there is a difference in meaning in so far as there was a difference in our points of view, and this would have become apparent had our talk proceeded, as it well might have done, thus:

* Cf. *the*, **85.**

87

Wife (to me): All you think about is your newspaper.
*Self: You worry too much. Who **did you think** it was?*

Chiefly interested in the paper before me, I had made the point
NOW my primary concern and used the pre-present accordingly.
Peter's mother, with her mind still on the moment in the past when
she had heard steps on the stairs, had made *that* her primary concern.

171.   The example just given should explain:

(*a*) **Who broke** *the window?* (The speaker has registered the fact
that now it is broken, but he is no longer interested in NOW. What
he wants to know is how the accident happened *when* it happened.)

(*b*) **Did you have** *a good journey?* (I'm glad to see you—you know
that. I am now thinking of the time in the past when you were on
your way here.)

In both those cases, aspect THREE would be equally acceptable;
e.g. *Oh, who has broken the window?* (I don't want to know how it
happened; the fact is that it is broken, and I'm asking who is re-
sponsible.) Similarly, with *today, this morning, this afternoon,* etc.,
both the FOURTH aspect (*it happened*) and the THIRD (*it has
happened*) are possible, according to whether SPPC is point NOW
or an earlier time in the period in question. Note:

(THIRD   (*a*) *Have you been very busy today* (during the period
aspect)   before now)?
          (*b*) *I have seen him this morning. I've just seen him*
                (at an unspecified time).
(FOURTH (*c*) *Your letter* **reached** *me this morning.* (Someone
aspect)   brought it at a definite moment earlier in the
                morning; or this morning if the morning has
                passed). **It arrived** *just now* (i.e. a moment ago).
          (*d*) *It* **was** *terribly hot in town today* (but it is cooler
                out here in the country, now).

172.   As in **171** (*d*), the FOURTH aspect can (but does not necessarily) indicate that former conditions no longer exist. Thus *He was
an excellent chairman* suggests that he is not chairman now. *He was
a wonderful man* suggests he is dead. The essential mark on the
FOURTH aspect is the idea of an interval between the point NOW
and the specific time of the event in which the speaker is interested.
Other examples: *Where were you born? I was born at ——;* and *We
enjoyed our stay immensely* (our stay ended, say, yesterday), but *We
have enjoyed our stay* (which is now ending).

173.   **167–172** could be summarised in the formula *pre-present v past* : : *unspecified time before now v specified time in the past, detached from now*; and in the diagram:

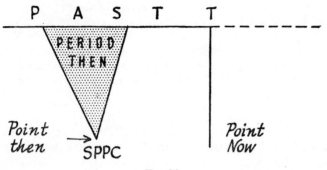

FIG. 24

THEN (past) can be any point or period of time in the past, however recent or distant, but the speaker must have some specific time in mind. THEN can move forwards as a series of events is reported, e.g. *Caesar came, (then) he saw, (then) he conquered.* It could be concentrated on a momentary action, or cover a narrow or a wide range of events.

174.   Examples:

   (I) *Point THEN*

(I O) (*a*) *What* **did I do** *in Example* **159** (*a*)*?* **I wrote** *the letter* '*e*'.
(I U) (*b*) *What* **was I doing** *then?* **I was writing.**

   (II) *Period THEN*

(I O) (*c*) **I lived** *in England when* **I was** *a boy.*
(S O) (*d*) **I got up** *early in those days.*
(I U) (*e*) **I was learning** *Arabic all last year; and*
(S U) (*f*) **I was** *then* **getting up** *at six o'clock in order to study it.*

Remember that examples (*b*), (*e*) and (*f*) are simply applications of the U aspect of activity to the past aspect of time: it is not necessary to explain them in terms of 'interruption' (see **33**).

175.   **I O** extending over a period, and **S O**, as in examples **174** (*c*) and (*d*), can be expressed by *used to*, when emphasis falls on the idea of an act continued or repeated over a period *in the past*, not in the present. E.g. **I used to live** *in England* (but I don't now); **I used to get**

up *early* (now I'm not so energetic). This emphatic marking would normally only occur once in a short sentence and would not fall on a verb in a subordinate position: thus, *I used to get up early when I went to school.* Note the interrogative and negative—*Used you to go? I used not to go.* These constructions are often felt to be pedantic, while *Did you use to go? I didn't use to go,* common enough in so-called uneducated speech, have not yet become respectable. We can avoid this dilemma by saying *Did you usually go? I never used to go.* Note that *I use to go (Present), though good Shakespearean English, is no longer current. Modern English would say *I usually go.*

(5) The Pre-past

176.   In our FIFTH aspect, **pre-past, S P P C** in Fig. 23 has turned backwards, and the pattern in Fig. 21 is applied to that in Fig. 24, thus:

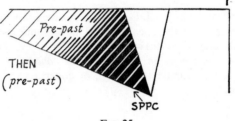

FIG. 25

The speaker's concern resembles that in **162**; i.e. it is either with activity performed or occurring within the period BEFORE THEN or in the period ending BY THEN; or it is with activity beginning in the past before **S P P C**, i.e. SINCE THEN (pre-past) and continuing till **S P P C**.

177.   Examples:

   (I) *Activity BEFORE THEN*

(I O)   (*a*)   *I hear you went to India last year.* **Had you** *ever* **been** *there before? Yes,* **I'd been** *there six years before.**

(I U)   (*b*)   *When I found the streets so wet, I naturally supposed it* **had been raining.**

(S O)   (*c*)   *The door-bell rang, but there was nobody there.* **That had** *already* **happened** *twenty times during the day.*

  * Not six years *ago,* which would mean 'measured back from the point NOW'.

(S U) (*d*) *The place looked very different.* **They had been building** *everywhere.*

(II) *Activity CONTINUING TILL THEN*

(**I O**) (*e*) *I sold my house last summer.* **I had lived** *in it for twelve years, ever since my father died.**

(**I U**) (*f*) *By the time I arrived in Egypt,* **I had been studying** *Arabic for eighteen months.*

(S O) (*g*) *Till then, I had usually* **got up** *at seven; but—*

(S U) (*h*) **I had been getting up** *at six in order to work at the language, so I arrived rather tired.*

178. In this aspect we are dealing with a *prelude* to the past and not merely with a sequence of past events. In *Caesar came, (then) he saw, (then) he conquered* or in *First he kissed me, then he left me,* **S P P C** moves forward with each event: one event may precede another, but that is not the essential point in the pre-past. This aspect is only adopted when the speaker has to make it clear, or wishes to emphasise the fact, that some action preceded **S P P C**. Thus, in **177** (*e*), *I had lived* is necessary to make it clear that the speaker is referring to the period prior to the sale, which is the **S P P C**; but where my father's death occurs in that order of events is obvious without the particular distinction contained in the prelude to the past—hence *my father died.* In **177** (*e*), therefore, **the past** is used both for what happened at **S P P C** (*I sold my house*) and for what had happened before then (*my father died*). In other words, in the pair *past v prelude to the past,* the latter is a marked form which need not be used unless emphasis or clarity demands it. Other examples:

(*a*) *The train left before I got to the station.* The order of events is clear. To emphasise it, I could say *the train had left*; and that construction might still be preferred by writers drilled in traditional grammar. But it would be pedantic to mark *the train left* 'wrong'.

(*b*) *When I arrived at the station I found the train had left (two minutes before).* Here *had left* would be required to make it clear that the train's departure on that occasion preceded my arrival, and especially to mark the idea of such-and-such a time *before.* Besides, *I found the train left two minutes before,* could mean that it usually left, or was scheduled to leave, two minutes before the time I arrived.

(*c*) *'As the Chairman told you, I was in Ghana,'* the lecturer began. The speaker's being in Ghana preceded the Chairman's remarks. However, not only is the order of events obvious to the audience,

* See **178**.

but the speaker's primary concern is with his stay in Ghana, and it is this that he is going to talk about.

(*d*) *I saw Michael on Sunday. He hadn't gone back to the office yet.* Here, *he hadn't gone back* is essential to the sense. *He didn't go back* would suggest that his non-return was the consequence of my seeing him; in any case, *yet* is not used with that aspect of time. *He hasn't gone back* would mean *by now*; but what the speaker meant was *by then*.

(6 & 7) The Continuation of the Present: the Future

179. Whereas the past is a chronicle of facts (i.e. things done) the future is a tale untold, a mirage of events unfulfilled. At its most certain, the future is the sphere of things we expect to happen. We *expect*, i.e. look out into the future and imagine something accomplished. The unreal world ahead of us is not defined nearly as sharply as the period before now. The English tense system reflects no clear division between post-present and future, comparable to the distinction between pre-present and past. *I'll go, I'm going*, and *I'm going to fly* could apply equally to indefinite time from now on and to specified time in the future. The problems of future tense in English involve not only aspects of activity and of time, but also MOODS, i.e. the certainty, hesitation, willingness, determination, hope, sense of obligation or of prohibition, or simply neutrality, with which the speaker views the unfulfilled event; and futurity can be expressed in a variety of ways in English accordingly. Moods will be discussed later. Meanwhile, to illustrate the combination of aspects of activity with future time, let us take the most neutral expression of futurity in English, the conversational *I'll*. The conversational rather than the written form is chosen because for many English speakers mood enters at once into the problem of *I will v I shall* with its countless personal, regional and contextual associations. (For contractions like *I'll*, see first footnote to **28**.)

180. Nevertheless, the ideas of **continuation of the present** (SIXTH aspect of time, Fig. 26) and **future** (SEVENTH aspect, Fig. 27) are capable of separate expression in English. They can always be distinguished by adverbials such as *from now on, henceforth* and *at some future date*.

Future time detached from now, as past time is detached from now, becomes apparent in **the pre-future** (see **183** and Fig. 28). Of the constructions *I'm leaving, I'm going to leave, I'll leave*, the first two are more suggestive of the present continued, the last of future detached from the present; but that does not account for all the difference.* *I am going to the bank tomorrow and will pay the cheque in then* means that arrangements for my going to the bank tomorrow

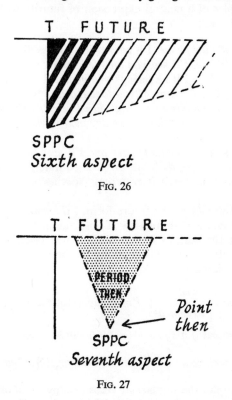

T FUTURE
SPPC
Sixth aspect

FIG. 26

T FUTURE
PERIOD THEN
Point then
SPPC
Seventh aspect

FIG. 27

are now made, and, at the time of my arrival, which is not yet, I will pay the cheque in: the mark of future time is on *will pay*. However, in that sentence we are also placing an emphasis (explained in **153**) on the first verb and do not feel it necessary to repeat the same emphasis on the second. If we did not want to give that emphasis at

* Note the interesting example given by R. W. Zandvoort in *A Handbook of English Grammar* (Longmans, Green & Co.), page 41. '*I'm not coming to this service,' William said to Charles and Rosamund. 'I shall catch crabs and filefish in the pools.*' Professor Zandvoort comments: '*I'm not coming to this service* expresses the speaker's determination *now*; *I shall catch crabs* denotes what he will do an hour hence.' However, there is also an element of *mood* in that *I shall catch crabs*. It strikes a note of anti-social defiance which would not be present in *I'm catching* or *I'll catch*.

all we could simply say *I'll go to the bank tomorrow and pay the money in.*

181.   Examples of a neutral expression of futurity with unspecified and specified time:

(I O) (*a*) *That's the phone.* **I'll answer** it. (Unspecified time)
     (*b*) *Good-bye.* **I'll see** *you on Wednesday.* (Specified)
(I U) (*c*) *Good-bye.* **I'll be seeing*** *you again.* (Unspecified)
     (*d*) **We'll be thinking** *of you tomorrow.* (Specified)
(S O) (*e*) **I'll get up** *late every day when I've retired.*†
(S U) (*f*) **I'll be working** *late every day next week.*

Compare *You answer that letter and* **I'll answer** *this one* and **I've answered** *that one already* (both unspecified time), with **I'll answer** *it tomorrow* and **I answered** *it yesterday* (specified).

182.   The examples of the future form, *I'll answer*, etc., in **181** are all marked from the point of view of *time*: the speaker is emphasising the fact that the act, so far unfulfilled, will occur in the future. Observe the absence of this marking in the subordinate clause in each of the following:

(*a*) **I'll come** $\begin{cases} when \\ as\ soon\ as \end{cases}$ *I'm ready.* (Not **when I'll be ready.*)

(*b*) **We'll go out** *if it's fine.* (Not **if it will be fine.*)

(*c*) **We'll stay** *indoors* $\begin{cases} until \\ unless \end{cases}$ *it stops raining.* (Not **until it will stop.*)

In these examples the unmarked verbs occupy a subordinate position in the sentence. This unmarked future is usually found in temporal and conditional clauses. But we cannot assume that absence of marking will be found exclusively or infallibly in such clauses: the criterion is whether or not the marking is essential to the meaning or is deliberately intended. Observe the marked form in:

(*d*) *I'll come, if* **it will** *help.* Here I am stressing the possibility of my presence helping on some future occasion. Observe also the difference between—

(*e*) *Tell me when you're ready;* and

---

* U aspect, suggesting the expected, uncompleted experience of being in your company. See also **207**, *c*.

† See **185**. Here, *I've retired* is unmarked in the pair *I've retired v I'll have retired.*

(*f*) *Tell me when* **you'll be** *ready.*

In (*e*), the situation is that you are not ready yet; and that *when* you are ready, I want you to tell me. In (*f*), I want you to tell me, now, *at what time in the future you will be ready.*

(8) The Pre-future

183.   The next aspect of time (the EIGHTH), **the prelude to the future,** is comparable with the other *preludes* (Figures 21 and 25) and could be illustrated thus:

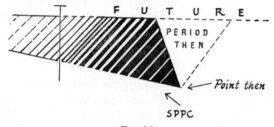

Fig. 28

The period which the speaker is now considering is imagined as viewed from some future time, detached from the present. That period may begin at any time before THEN (future), either in the pre-future or before the momentary present. In other words, the period may or may not have already begun at the time of speaking.

184.   Examples:

(I O)   (*a*) *I haven't answered the letter yet, but* **I'll have done** *so by Friday.* (On Friday I'll be able to look back and see that *it has been answered.*)

(*b*) *I started writing this book six months ago. By the end of this week,* **I'll have written** 200 *pages.*

(I U)   (*c*) *By then,* **I'll have been writing** *this book for just over six months.*

(S O)   (*d*) *By the end of the year, the moon* **will have gone** *round the earth thirteen times.*

(S U)   (Examples possible but rare.)

185.   *I'll have done, I'll have written,* etc., are *marked* forms essential to the meaning or deliberately intended. In **184** (*a*), *I'll answer it by Friday* is possible but does not give the emphasis explained in the

parenthesis. A similar remark would apply to (*d*) if the statement in (*d*) were made early in January. In (*b*) and (*c*), where the period begins before now, *I'll have written* and *I'll have been writing*, are essential to the sense. Observe the *unmarked* form, similar to that in **181** (*e*) (*when I've retired*): in writing the parenthesis to **184** (*a*), I automatically used the unmarked form *it has been answered*. I could have used a marked form and said: *I can then make sure that it will have been answered*. Even then, it is interesting to note that in shifting the emphasis in this way I avoided using two marked forms in the sentence—*I'll be able* (mark on future) *to see that it will have been answered* (mark on pre-future) is clumsy. The unmarked pre-future is usual in temporal or conditional clauses, e.g. *I'll get up late, when I've retired*, and *I'll telephone him as soon as I've finished my breakfast.*

(9) The Future in the Past

186. For this, the NINTH aspect, the speaker's point of primary concern is in the past and his vision is directed forwards, to the more recent past, to the present or into the actual future, like this:

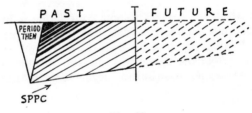

FIG. 29

187. This aspect of time occurs to the speaker when he is reporting, from a point of view in the past, the kind of situation reflected in the examples in **181** and **182**. Example:

I said (thought, told you, etc.)
- **I'd answer** (i) *it.*
- **I'd see** *you on Wednesday.*
- **I'd be seeing** *you again.*
- **we'd be thinking** *of you the next day* (ii).
- **I'd get up** *late when I'd retired* (iii).
- **I'd be working** *late every day the following week* (iv).

$$I \text{ said } \textbf{I'd come} \begin{cases} \textit{when (as soon as) I was ready.} \\ \textit{if it was fine.} \end{cases}$$

We said **we'd stay** *indoors, until (unless) it stopped raining.*
I promised you **I'd come,** *if* **it would** (v) **be** *any help.*

$$I \text{ asked you to tell me} \begin{cases} \textit{when you were ready.} \\ \textit{when } \textbf{you'd be} \textit{ ready (vi).} \end{cases}$$

188.   Notes on **187**:

(i) The 'neutral' conversational form *I'd*, corresponding to *I'll* in **179**, would be expressed in formal written language as *I would* or *I should*.

(ii) *Tomorrow*, being the day after the point NOW, is impossible here, except in the situation described in **189**.

(iii) *I'd* (*i.e. I had*) *retired*—an unmarked* expression for the pre-future as seen from the past: cf. **181** (*e*). However, *I've retired* would also be possible, as explained in **189**. Distinguish between *I'd* (I had) *retired* and *I'd* (I would or should) *retire*.

(iv) Not *next week*, which is the week following the present one, except in the situation described in **189**.

(v) and (vi)—Cf. **182** (*d*) and (*f*).

189.   *It would be* can express the idea of futurity from a past viewpoint, even if part of the future thus seen happens to correspond with the period after point NOW; in other words, even if in Fig. 29 we go past **T**. This supports the traditional 'rule' about the sequence of tenses which insists on *he says it will be* but *he said it would be*. Nevertheless, if we do go past **T** in Fig. 29, it would not be illogical, nor contrary to widespread usage, to say

$$I \text{ said} \begin{cases} (a) \textit{ I'll answer it.} \\ (b) \textit{ I'll see you on Wednesday.} \\ (c) \textit{ I'll be seeing you again.} \\ (d) \textit{ we'll be (or we'd be) thinking of you tomorrow.} \\ (e) \textit{ I'll (or I'd) get up late when I've retired.} \\ (f) \textit{ I'll be (or I'd be) working late next week.} \\ (g) \textit{ I'll (or I'd) come as soon as I'm ready.} \end{cases}$$

In (*d*), (*e*), (*f*) and (*g*), it would be understood by a native-English hearer that the speaker must be referring to time after point NOW if he said *tomorrow, when I've retired, next week* and *as soon as I'm ready*.

* The marked equivalent is *I'd* (i.e. I would or should) *have retired.*

190. Thus in referring to time extending beyond **T**, the speaker might say **I'll** or **I'd**. Which is 'right'? The only answer of practical value would be that produced by an examination of many examples of acceptable usage. However, I do not consider it unjustifiable to regularise my own usage, in deliberate speech or writing, in accordance with my personal conception of the underlying system of English; and this is no doubt a justification for prescriptive grammar. I would therefore maintain (consistently, I hope, with the argument in this book) that *I said I'll see you on Wednesday* involves a sudden switch of **S P P C** from the past to point **NOW** or point **THEN** (future), and that such a switch in the middle of a (short) sentence is to be avoided, unless the speaker intends it to give emphasis to the fact that the future seen from the past is not yet fulfilled but will be so. *I said I'll see you on Wednesday* would in any case be acceptable if what the speaker means could be written *I said, 'I'll see you on Wednesday.'*

191. It is possible to express a *continuation of the past* comparable to a continuation of the present. This is fairly easily seen in

(*a*) *What were we doing* (**I U**, past aspect) *last lesson? You were telling us* (**I U**, past aspect) *about X and then* **you were going** (continuation of the past) *to tell us about Y.*

It is not so easily seen with

(*b*) *George dropped in yesterday evening, just for a chat.* **We were dining** *at the Jones's, but he simply wouldn't go, so we were terribly late.*

In (*b*), *we were dining* is a past equivalent of *we are dining*, i.e. *we have been invited to dine, have accepted and expect to be there* (**153**). In certain circumstances, there could even be a past equivalent of *We sail at some future time.* For instance, *we sailed at three* could mean that we were due to sail at some time after **S P P C**, e.g. *We really couldn't lunch with you on our last day. We sailed at three and had so much to do before we left.*

The Tenses

192. The tenses are thus verbal forms and constructions which express aspects of activity combined with aspects of time. They are not the only expressions of aspects of activity (see Chapter Eight) and aspects of time can be expressed by other means when the tense remains unaltered, as in *we sail tomorrow* and the historic present.

193. The various tenses of the verb *ask*, for example, in the **active** voice, are set out below, with names that are commonly attached to them:

Aspect of time	Aspect of activity	Example	Tense
1. Undivided; and	O	I ask	Present Simple*
2. Present	U	I am asking	Present Continuous
3. Pre-present	O	I have asked	Present Perfect
	U	I have been asking	Present Perfect Continuous
4. Past	O	I asked†	Past Simple
	U	I was asking	Present Continuous
5. Pre-past	O	I had asked	Present Perfect
	U	I had been asking	Present Perfect Continuous
6. Continuation of present	O U	} I am going to ask‡	(No traditional name but commonly classified as 'Future')
7. Future	O	I'll ask	Future Simple
	U	I'll be asking	Future Continuous
8. Pre-future	O	I'll have asked	Present Perfect
	U	I'll have been asking	Present Perfect Continuous
9. Future seen from the past	O	I'd ask	Future-in-the-Past
	U	I'd be asking	

The traditional names could perhaps be simplified and made more applicable to modern usage, as follows:

		New name
1 and 2.	I ask	**Present**
	I am asking	Present Continuous
3.	I have asked	**Pre-present**
	I have been asking	Pre-present Continuous
4.	I asked, I used to ask	**Past**
	I was asking	Past Continuous
5.	I had asked	**Pre-past**
	I had been asking	Pre-past Continuous
6.	I am going to ask	**Future**
7.	I'll ask	

* The so-called 'simple' tenses are, by comparison with the 'continuous' ones, unmarked.

† Note also *used to ask* (**175**), which has in effect become a tense form.

‡ The U aspect can be expressed, e.g. *I'm going to be asking a lot of questions at the meeting this afternoon.*

	I'll be asking	Future Continuous
8.	I'll have asked	**Pre-future**
	I'll have been asking	Pre-future Continuous
9.	I'd ask ⎱	**Future-in-the-Past**
	I'd be asking ⎰	

194.   The **passive** voice* can be similarly expressed:

1 and 2.	I am asked
3.	I have been asked
4.	I was asked
5.	I had been asked
6.	I am going to be asked
7.	I'll be asked
8.	I'll have been asked
9.	I'd be asked

In the passive the **U** aspect is generally found only in the Present (*I am being asked*) and the Past (*I was being asked*), although I have heard educated native-English speakers say *He'll be being interviewed on Friday.*

195.   The Conditional, with its **O** and **U** aspects, active and passive, will be treated under **MOOD**, in Chapter Nine. In form it resembles the Future in the Past.

196.   The functions of the tenses set out in **193** and **194** should be clear from what has been said under **ACTIVITY** and **TIME** earlier in this chapter. They are summarised and further explained in the following paragraphs.

Present Tense

197.   This tense is used for—
(*a*) aspects of activity **A**, **I O** and **S O** in both time undivided and

---

* The passive plays an important part in English usage, but the questions it raises are of a different order, I feel, from those with which I am chiefly concerned in this book. Students would be well advised to observe how the passive is used in English, with the effect, for example, (*a*) of emphasising the person or thing to whom or to which an action is directed, (*b*) of omitting mention of the agent when that is unimportant or irrelevant, or (*c*) of shifting the responsibility for an action away from the real initiator of it. Students will have no difficulty in finding examples of (*a*) and (*b*). Examples of (*c*) are very common in spoken English, e.g. *What time are we expected this evening?* In that instance, *our host* is expecting us, but our primary concern in that utterance is what we ourselves will do.

time present. Observe how the Present is used when an action is seen synoptically or in a static picture: e.g. *We climb the mountain* (chapter heading describing the action seen as a whole); *Aeneas carries his father out of the burning city* (caption describing a picture); Hamlet wounds Laertes (from a commentary on *Hamlet*, or from the synopsis of it);

(*b*) uncompleted action, when the speaker does not wish to stress the U aspect or when the emphasis on the U aspect is required elsewhere; e.g. *'Now we're moving'* **say** *the passengers as the ship at last* **draws** *away from the quay*. Stylistically a rhythmical alternation of marked and unmarked forms may be desirable, as it is with stressed words and syllables;

(*c*) future action, seen as accomplished; e.g. *Tomorrow I cross the Rubicon* (one can imagine this being said, dictatorially, by a Julius Caesar); or *We leave at 8.15* (in accordance with a definite time-table);

(*d*) future action reported in a subordinate position; e.g. in conditional and temporal clauses, unless the idea of future time is specially marked (see **182**);

(*e*) past action, envisaged as completed in present time, i.e. the historic present, used in story-telling for dramatic effect.

Present Continuous

198. Used for:

(*a*) **I U** or **S U** in both time undivided and time present. See **197** (*b*). The Present Continuous is a marked form used when the speaker is concerned with the fact that the action is in progress or that the subject of the verb is engaged in that action. Since the Present Continuous is a commentary on action in progress, it is best illustrated not by a static picture but by a moving one, as in a moving film or on television. Remember that some acts, by their nature, are not easily or normally envisaged in an uncompleted state: they may take place too quickly, or it may be difficult for the actor to prevent or suspend accomplishment. This would affect **I U**, but not **S U**.

(*b*) Future action, whether imagined as uncompleted or as accomplished, which is in any case uncompleted in the sense that it has been planned or arranged but is not yet fulfilled. Ordinary human beings unlike Julius Caesar, might say *We're crossing the Rubicon tomorrow*.

Pre-present

199. For **I O** and **S O** in the prelude to the present. Note that:

(*a*) the speaker may be considering activity accomplished before now, or activity continuing till now (**162** and **163**), the time of the action being, in either case, unspecified;

(*b*) the speaker may be conscious of the present result of this activity and it may be the result which makes him think of the act which has produced it; but this, though important, is an *incidental* factor, not the essential one;

(*c*) since it refers to time before *point NOW*, the Pre-present can be used when we have in mind the first half of *period NOW* (see **160,** Fig. 20). Thus, *He sits here, hour after hour, brooding over his misfortunes* could be divided into two parts, corresponding to the two halves of the triangle in Fig. 20—(i) *He has sat here, hour after hour*, and (ii) *He will sit here, hour after hour*;

(*d*) this tense is used as an unmarked form, in a subordinate position in the sentence, of the Pre-future (see **185**).

Pre-present Continuous

200. For **I U** and **S U** in the prelude to the present. Here we are simply transferring to time before now the idea behind the Present Continuous so that *You are reading this book now* becomes *You have been reading it before or until now*. Remember that the action, being uncompleted, may or may not continue into the present (see **165,** Fig. 22).

Past

201. Used for:

(*a*) **I O** and **S O** in the past, when the time of the action is specified, or imagined by the speaker to be detached from the present;

(*b*) an unmarked substitute for the Pre-past (see **178,** *a* and *c*);

(*c*) occasionally as a past equivalent of the usage in **197** (*c*); e.g. *we* **sailed,** meaning that we were due to sail, *at 8.15.*

202. The form of the past tense is also used in subordinate clauses containing the idea of

(*a*) an act not fulfilled but desirable, e.g. *Hurry up. It's time* **we left.** *I wish* **I knew** (now) *what the answer* **was** (now); and

(*b*) an act not fulfilled but supposed, e.g. *I don't smoke; but if* **I did,** *I would smoke a pipe.*

In these examples, *I left, I knew* and *I did* are not really in the past tense but are expressions of *mood* (see Chapter Nine, paragraph **238**). Note the special case of *were*, in

I'm not rich—I wish I were.
He's not either. If he were, he wouldn't be here.

In the last two examples, *were* indicates something not only unfulfilled but contrary to reality.

Past Continuous

203. Used for:

(*a*) **I U** and **S U** in the past. Here we have a transfer into the past of the idea behind the Present Continuous so that *You are reading this book now* becomes *You were reading it* (five minutes ago);

(*b*) sometimes as a past equivalent of the usage in **198** (*b*): see the example given in **191** (*b*). Observe that whereas the dictator might say *I cross the Rubicon tomorrow* and the ordinary mortal *I am crossing it tomorrow*, an undecided man, if asked 'What are you doing tomorrow?' might answer, '*Er-well—I was crossing the Rubicon*'—i.e. I was thinking of crossing it before you asked me, but now I am willing to do whatever you suggest;

(*c*) **U** applied to the ideas in **202**:

It's time we were leaving.

I wish I was (or *were*) *going with you tomorrow.*

If you were looking after yourself properly, you wouldn't catch cold so often.

Pre-past

204. Used for **I O** and **S O**:

(*a*) as an equivalent in the pre-past either of (i) the Pre-present or (ii) of the Past. Example:

(i) *We are too late—the train has gone* (**S P P C** at point **NOW**). *We arrived too late—the train had gone* (**S P P C** at point **THEN**, the time of our arrival).

(ii) *I posted your letter on my way to the office* (**SPPC** at the time of posting the letter). *I had already posted it when I got your message telling me you didn't want it to go* (**S P P C** at time of receiving the message).

Note that in (*ii*) the Pre-past is a marked form which is only required when, for the sake of emphasis or clarity, it is necessary to specify that certain action preceded **S P P C**. When that specification is unnecessary or irrelevant, the Past Tense may be used, as in **178** (*a*) and (*c*).

(*b*) as an unmarked expression, in a subordinate position in the sentence, of the Pre-future as seen from the past (**188**, note *iii*).

(*c*) as a past equivalent of the idea contained in **202**, especially when it is clear that the event was not fulfilled:

I wish **I had known** (then) *what the answer was.*

If **I had been** *a smoker, I would have smoked a pipe.*

103

English as a Foreign Language

Pre-Past Continuous

205.   Used for **I U** and **S U** in the situations given in **204**.

Future

206.   (*a*) Although in certain usages *I am doing* and *I am going to do* appear to express the post-present, and *I'll do* the future detached from the present, all three constructions can express **I O** and **S O** in both aspects of time and might be classified as Future Tenses.

> *I'll see him*
> *I'm seeing him* ⎫ *from now on, or tomorrow afternoon.*
> *I'm going to see him* ⎭

(*b*) The *going to* form of the Future is characteristic of colloquial English and would usually be avoided in formal writing where *will* or *shall* would be preferred or even considered obligatory. In colloquial English, *I am going to see* is commonly used in a stressed position* in the sentence as a mark of emphasis on present conditions, e.g. intentions or indications, leading to future action (see **155**). If such emphasis is required in formal writing, one would use an expression like *I intend*, or *have arranged, have an appointment* or *am certain to see*.

(*c*) At the same time, *I'll see*, though it bears the mark of future time, lacks the emphasis just referred to. Note the presence or absence of this emphasis in the following examples:

(i) (The telephone rings) *All right, I'll answer it.* (The situation does not require the emphasis. *I'm going to answer it* would suggest a sequence of consideration, decision, action and ultimate fulfilment, by the end of which the caller would have lost patience and rung off.)

(ii) *I'm going to answer your letter, point by point.* (Here the sequence of forethought, purpose, action and fulfilment is deliberately stressed.)

(iii) *I'll answer it if you give me time* (the conditions which might lead to future action are not provided).

(iv) *I don't like this car. I'm going to sell it.* (This breaks the news of my considered intentions and their consequence. Cf. *I think*

---

* Stress frequently produces analysis or 'breaking' in English. Cf. the unstressed verb in *I'll explain it in a moment*, and the stressed analytical construction in *Let me make this quite clear.*

I'll sell it, where the idea of intention is absent; or *I'll sell it for 400 pounds,* where emphasis is on the price.)

(v) *Tomorrow is going to be a busy day* (so much has been planned, all the evidence points to it). *Yes, it will be a busy day* (emphasis not repeated).

(vi) *Tomorrow will be Tuesday* (simple statement of future, with no justification for the stressed form).

(vii) *I'm going to read your essay this evening and I'll discuss it with you tomorrow* (emphasis on the first action, not repeated on the second).

(viii) (*I don't know the answer.*) *I'll know it next week.* (In such a case, not only does emphasis fall on the point in future time, but the idea of purpose, action and fulfilment would be irrelevant with such an act of perception (see **150, 154**). It would not be irrelevant in *I don't know the answer but I'm going to find out.*

(*d*) Note *He will sit here, hour after hour* (**199**, *c*, *ii*). This usage may also, but not necessarily, contain an element of mood. In any case, here it refers to repeated or continued action in present time.

(*e*) For subtleties of mood expressed by *shall* and *will*, see Chapter Nine.

Future Continuous

207. (*a*) **I U** and **S U** in future time can be expressed by the Future Continuous (*I'll be reading*). An emphasis similar to that in **206** (*b*) is found in *I'm going to be reading.*

(*b*) The Future Continuous is often used to make it clear that a process has not yet started: *I'll be crossing the Rubicon tomorrow* (cf. **198**, *b*). Note the considerate application of this in *Will you be passing the post-office?* (I know you are busy and may have other plans at the moment, but at some future time . . . ?)

(*c*) It is also used to mark the absence of the mood expressed by *shall/will* + infinitive (**226**). Thus *I'll be passing the post-office anyway* can be a plain statement of fact, uncoloured by mood—the future equivalent of *I'm passing the post-office at this moment.*

Pre-future and Pre-future Continuous

208. **I O** and **S O** and **I U** and **S U**, applied to the pre-future. Note that in a subordinate position in the sentence, the first of these two tenses would be replaced by the Pre-present, and the second by the Pre-present Continuous; e.g. *At the end of the week, I'll stop work and revise what I've done* (or *what I've been doing*).

Future-in-the-Past

209.   (*a*) **I O**, **S O**, **I U** and **S U** applied to the future as seen from the past.

(*b*) Transferred to past time, the example in **206** (*d*) becomes *He would sit here, hour after hour*. In this usage there is often an element of mood (see **237**). It refers to repeated or continued action in past time. Contrast this with *used to*, **175**.

SEQUENCES OF TENSES

210.   The question of which combination of tenses should be used in English in a piece of consecutive speech or writing is primarily a matter of deciding which tense is suitable for each separate action; and that, as we have seen earlier in this chapter, depends on the aspect of activity and the aspect of time with which the speaker is concerned, and on whether a marked or unmarked form is required. Take care of each tense, therefore, and the sequence will usually take care of itself. Since sudden and too frequent changes of point of primary concern are undesirable unless deliberately intended, Present Tenses tend to be found with Present, Pre-present and Future, while Past Tenses tend to be found with Past, Pre-past and Future-in-the-Past. Note the usages, in subordinate positions in the sentence, in **181** (*e*), **182** (*a*), (*b*) and (*c*), **184** (*a*) and **188** (*iii*). These remarks apply even to indirect speech, which is not subject to any special 'rules' of tense sequence. Certain conventional patterns are found in sentences containing conditional clauses (see **247**); but this does not exclude the possibility of having any combination of tenses, even in conditional sentences, if the meaning demands it.

CHAPTER EIGHT

Other Aspects of Activity

211. As well as the aspects of activity reflected in the Tenses, the speaker may be concerned with:

(*a*) the prelude of the act;
(*b*) the beginning of the process;
(*c*) the end of the process;
(*d*) the continuation of the activity;
(*e*) the completion of the act, as distinct from the act as a whole; or intensification of the act;
(*f*) the direction given to the act;
(*g*) the result of the act.

212. An example of **211** (*a*) is *get* as distinct from *have*. In formal language and with refinements of meaning, this distinction could be accentuated by the use of such words as *obtain* or *acquire* on the one hand, and *possess* or *occupy* on the other. It is difficult to see when *getting* ends and *having* begins; and if I have got something it is almost sure to follow that I have it. In colloquial English, *I've got* commonly replaces the weaker sounding *I have*, to indicate possession. But when the speaker clearly has in mind the having rather than the getting, as in *We have three weeks' holiday every year*, *I've got* does not, in the English to which the author is accustomed, replace *I have*.*

213. Other common expressions for the prelude to the act are *come to* (unstressed *to*) and *begin to*; e.g. *When we start thinking of these problems, we come to* (or *begin to*) *realise how complicated they are*. This device is frequently used with acts of perception, such as *see* and *know*, since it is easier to contemplate the prelude to an act of

---

* I have taken this example from Kruisinga's *Handbook of Present-Day English*. Kruisinga made one of the few errors in this prodigious work in explaining it by the argument that the perfect of *get* is not iterative. *I've got* can certainly be used for repeated action when we have in mind repeated getting; e.g. *Wonderful. You've got a bull's-eye every time* (shooting at a target).

perception, the effort of trying to perceive, than the act itself, which often suddenly happens, we know not how. (Cf. *I can see*, **261**.)

214.   *Start* (*think*)*ing* is one way of indicating the beginning of the process; *stop* (*think*)*ing*, the end of it. Note the verb-form ending in *-ing* indicating the process itself, as we saw in the previous chapter. Thus a complete act, described synoptically by the **O** form (e.g. *go*), can be seen analytically in its **U** form (*going*); the first part of *going* would be *starting* (which I feel to express physical movement, whereas *beginning* is more neutral, and *commencing* more abstract and formal). We *start off, start out, set off, set out* (for this use of *off* and *out*, see **343**). At the end of the process, we *get to* and finally *arrive at* our destination.

215.   Continuation of the process is indicated by *go on* (*walk*)*ing*, *keep* (*walk*)*ing*, *keep on* (*walk*)*ing*. The same construction indicates the continuation of a series of completed acts: *They keep sending my letters to the wrong address.*

216.   The completion of the act, as distinct from the act itself, is marked in such pairs as *wake v wake 'up, drink v drink 'up, eat v eat 'up*. The verbs *eat* and *drink* can therefore be found in all the following aspects:

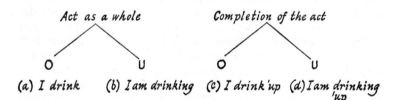

Examples of (*c*) *and* (*d*): *Drink up your medicine. I am drinking it up*, i.e. I am in process of completing the act. We can also say *I am drinking it down*, with similar meaning, but see **218**.

217.   The *up*, especially in the imperative, often acts as a spur to the activity, as in *Hurry 'up*. But note that in the negative, *Don't hurry*, we are concerned with the act itself, not with the completion or the intensification of it. Note also the contrast between the completion of an act and the reversal of an act, already completed, in *tie up* (a shoe-lace) or *untie* (*it*), and many similar examples.

OTHER ASPECTS OF ACTIVITY

218. The *drink 'up* pattern also serves to give a more intensive or a specialised meaning to the plain verb, as in *to look up a word in the dictionary, to call up a friend on the telephone, to work out a problem, to find out the answer*. Again, it serves to indicate the direction taken by an action; *give 'out* or *hand 'out the examination papers* (distribute them from a central point), *give* (or *hand*) *them 'in* (to a central point). Similarly, *give 'back, put 'on, take 'off, break 'down, bring 'along, hand 'over;* and *drink it 'down*, i.e. swallow it.

219. With a feeling for the aspects of activity in **211** (*e*) and (*f*), the student may be better able to distinguish the *drink 'up* pattern from the patterns exemplified in *'look at your 'book* and *'go to the 'door*. In all the expressions in **216, 217** and **218**—and there are many others like them—the particles, *up, out*, etc., can be separated from the verb and placed after the direct object. Thus:

(*a*) *Give out the examination papers* (emphasis on *papers*).

(*b*) *Give the examination papers 'out* (emphasis on distribution). There is no alternative word-order in:

(*c*) *Give them 'out*,

i.e. when the direct object is a pronoun, and when it does not therefore receive the emphasis made in (*a*). Note that, if separated from the verb, the particle, being emphasised, receives a strong stress; and that it must follow the direct object immediately without the intervention of an adverbial expression, thus

(*d*) *Look this word 'up in the dictionary*.

On the other hand, expressions like *look at, look for, ask for, talk about* cannot be split up by a direct object (*'look at it*), although they can be separated by an adverbial expression (*look in the 'cupboard for it*). In *look at, look for*, etc., the *at, for*, etc., serve as prepositions which must come before the direct object, just as in *go to the 'door* the preposition *to* must stand before the noun it governs. This will be further discussed in Chapter Eleven.

220. The result of activity, as distinct from the activity itself, is marked in the pair *do v make*, as in the following idiomatic phrases:

Activity	Result
do good, do harm	*make peace, make trouble, make war*
do your best	*make mistakes, make money*
do your duty	*don't make a noise*
do very good work	*make a useful contribution*

CHAPTER NINE

Auxiliary and Modal Verbs

Do

221. *Do, does* and *did* are used—

(*a*) to form the negative and interrogative of 'full verbs' (i.e. all except the auxiliary and modal verbs, which are discussed in this chapter); and

(*b*) to provide one of the two emphatic forms of 'full verbs'. Examples of these emphatic forms are—

(i) *I* **write** *my letters, I never type them* (stress on *write*).

(ii) *Who said I don't write them? I* **do** *write them* (emphasis on the positive as contrasted with the negative).

Be, Have, etc., to form Tenses

222. *Be, have,* and their various parts (*am, is, are, was, were, being, been, had*) and *used to* are used as *auxiliaries* to make up the tenses (see Chapter Seven). So are *will, shall, would* and *should,* although there is also a strong element of *mood* in these words, as we shall see below. Mood can be defined as an attitude towards activity. The speaker can regard activity as fulfilled or as certain to be fulfilled, in which case he is concerned with fact. Or he can be considering unfulfilled activity, i.e. non-fact. *Modal verbs* chiefly *express attitudes to unfulfilled activity. Want, wish, hope* and other verbs also express attitudes to unfulfilled activity. But modal verbs are peculiar in that, like the auxiliaries, they adopt the following pattern in the interrogative, negative and third person singular of the affirmative: *Must you? You must not* (*mustn't*). *Must you not* (*mustn't you?*). *He must.* They could be divided into four groups:

(*a*) *will, shall, would, should,* (which look forward from the **SPPC**);
(*b*) *should, ought to, must, have to, am to* (concerned with obligation);
(*c*) *can, could, may, might* (concerned with freedom to act);
(*d*) *dare, need.*

Will *v* Shall

223. These two words are associated with activity not fulfilled but imagined as fulfilled in time to come. An excessive amount of time in the teaching of English is spent on rules for the use of *will* and *shall*. Teachers are apt to regard mastery of these rules as essential to a command of English. Yet no part of English grammar is less amenable to rules than this, not only because of the subtleties involved, but also because usage varies from region to region in the English-speaking world, and from one individual speaker to another. The teaching of grammarians on these points is often contradicted in actual speech by the grammarians themselves. Moreover, there are circumstances in which either *shall* or *will* can be used, and good writers often exercise this option for reasons of style.

224. There are two prescriptive rules which are so widespread that they are bound to determine usage to a considerable extent, especially in English deliberately composed. These are:

(*a*) *Prescriptive rule for the plain future uncoloured by the speaker's mood:*

	Singular	Plural
1st Person	I shall	we shall
2nd Person	you will	you will
3rd Person	he, she, it will	they will

Example: *Tomorrow will be my birthday. I shall be fifty-one.* My feelings in the matter, whatever they may be, cannot alter the course of events.

(*b*) *Prescriptive rule for the future which reflects the speaker's will, command or prohibition:*

I will	we will
you shall	you shall
he, she, it shall	they shall

Example: *I will be obeyed, and you shall not ignore my wishes.* My feelings will determine what happens to me and to others.

225. These rules are useful guides and will take most students as far as they need to go in their own use of the language. But they so often fail to reflect the usage of distinguished writers, let alone of the average educated native-speaker, that the teacher should not attach too much importance to them, and the enquiring student might

demand something more satisfactory. To clear away the tangle of idiomatic and conflicting usage among native-speakers, with a view to discovering whatever underlying law might determine the use of *will* and *shall* in modern English, would be a wearisome and not very profitable labour. Meanwhile, in deciding which of these two words to use, we are bound either to accept the rules in **224,** with or without exceptions, or to adopt some other hypothesis.

226.   One hypothesis, following the lines of this book, and based on habits of speech with which I happen to be familiar, would be that *will* is the normal and *shall* the marked form of the auxiliary which makes up the Future Tense. A weak, unmarked *will* expresses a neutral future (see **179,** end) and makes a simple statement about the shape of things to come. The marked *shall* expresses various self-conscious attitudes towards the future—e.g. modesty, deference, decision, defiance—without a positive assurance as to the result. On the other hand, the strong *will* states the result positively, the speaker drawing a confident conclusion from his own or someone else's wishes or intentions, or from the evidence before him. Note that the strong *will*, emphasising the future event, can be contrasted not only with *shall* in this way, but also with *going to* (see **155**) which places its emphasis on the present indications of what the future will bring. *Will v shall* can thus be summarised:

Unmarked	*Marked*
WILL	SHALL
1. (weak) neutral future	Various self-conscious attitudes
2. (strong) giving a positive assurance about a future event	towards the unfulfilled event, without a positive assurance as to the outcome

227.   While *shall* is often used in the neutral future for the first person singular and plural for the reasons given in **224** and **232,** *will* tends to be used for every person, including the first. In any case, in fluent speech, the neutral future is commonly expressed in the first person by *I'll* and *we'll*. In the positive future, the tendency to use *will* for every person, including the first, is particularly strong.

228.   Examples of the neutral future:

(*a*) *I'll probably be home late this evening.* Here, *I'll* could be replaced by *I will* or *I shall*.

(*b*) *You will be glad to hear the news* (no alternative to *will*).

(*c*) *Where there is most confidence, there will be most freedom* (no alternative).

229.   Examples of the positive future:

(*a*) *We WILL find a Cure for Cancer if* . . . This was the heading of an appeal in a London newspaper (*The Observer*, 13 December 1959). The text beneath explained that 'if the necessary help is provided the cure will certainly be found'. *Shall* would also have been possible here, but then the particular emphasis made by the obviously deliberate use of *will* would have been lost.

(*b*) The marriage vow, *I will*. This is a promise, i.e. a confident statement about the future, based on the speaker's firm intention. In this particular instance, *shall* is not used.

(*c*) *Let our motto be 'I will not be afraid'*. (From the Christmas message by King George VI, December 1950.) Here *shall* would be too diffident, but not unacceptable.

(*d*) *He will do what I tell him*. (A command so confident that it becomes a positive, objective statement of fact: cf. **231**, *c*, iv.)

(*e*) Note the contrast with *going to*:

A. *I think it's going to rain.*
B. *It looks like it, but you can't be sure.*
A. *I bet you it will rain.*

230.   Wish is evident in invitations such as

(*a*) *Will you have some more tea?* when the speaker is asking about your present wishes and future action. In—

(*b*) *Will you post this letter for me?* the speaker is expressing his own wishes and making a request.

(*c*) *He 'WILL sit there—I keep asking him not to* expresses wilfulness on his part. *He won't move* expresses refusal. The reader could find examples, especially in literature, of *will* as an expression of volition, but he should beware of using *will* as a substitute for *want to* or *intend to*. In (*a*), (*b*) and (*c*), *will* is not replaceable by *shall*. Note that *will you be having*, etc., is a plain reference to future activity (**207**, *c*).

231.   *Shall* could be considered as a mark of

(*a*) *modesty*, when the speaker is talking about his own future actions. This is especially noticeable in formal correspondence, where it is felt, by some, that *I shall* is more politely unassuming, *I will* is brusque and more self-assertive. This show of modesty would have been out of place in the motto quoted in **229** (*c*). However, in the plain prose of letter-writing, *I shall arrive next Monday* and *I will arrive next Monday* are both acceptable English, the choice between them being a matter of taste, habit or chance;

(*b*) *deference*, when the speaker is asking about the wishes of the person addressed, e.g.

(i) *Shall I open the window?* (i.e. do you want me to open it? *Will I open . . . ?* might mean *Is that what will happen?*)
(ii) *Shall we go, or do you want to stay longer?*
(iii) *Shall the waiter serve coffee now?* (this is rarer than (*i*) and (*ii*), and would often be replaced by *Do you want* (or *would like*) *the waiter to serve . . . ?*);

(*c*) *determination* on the part of the speaker as to the course of future events. A perfect example of this is the defiant

(i) *They shall not pass,*

which was the English translation of the slogan of the French army defending Verdun during the First World War. *They will not pass,* though grammatically acceptable, loses the spirit of glorious defiance. The speaker's attitude here is almost the opposite of the modesty in (*a*), though it is none the less subjective. The difference between the modest *shall* and the defiant *shall* is often apparent in pronunciation. The former tends to be weak [ʃəl], with an apologetic hushed *sh* sound; the latter tends towards an emphatic [ʃæl], with a *sh* sound as in *shout*. Indeed, if this emphasis is not made in pronunciation, the force of *shall* as a gesture of defiance is lost. Other examples of the determined *shall* are

(ii) *I shall catch crabs* (see footnote to **180**). *I shall go my own way—you can't stop me.* There is a note of self-centred obstinacy in these examples.
(iii) *You shall have whatever you want—I promise you that.* Compare the tone of the promise here with **229** (*b*).
(iv) *He shall do what I tell him.* Here the speaker's command is pompous, and the outcome not so certain as in **229** (*d*).
(v) *There shall be no more wars:* a wise decree that does not give an assurance that *wars will never occur again.*

232. After *we*, *shall* may be preferred to *will* for the sake of euphony. The deliberate use of *we will* can be very effective, as in the example

in **229** (*a*). But *w—w*—requires deliberate pronunciation; it is not easy in fluent speech and unless intended it may 'sound wrong' to the native-speaker.

Will have, shall have

233.   *I will have done, I shall have done,* etc., form the Pre-future Tense (see **183** and **208**). The criteria for the use of *will* and *shall* in this tense are similar to those in the foregoing paragraphs.

Would *v* Should

234.   *Would* and *should* are subject to the same sort of flexibility as *will* and *shall.* The two pairs are comparable, though not exactly parallel at every point; and *would* is not always the past equivalent of *will,* nor *should* of *shall.*

235.   *Would* and *should* may be considered as past equivalents of *will* and *shall* when used to make up the *Future-in-the-Past Tense* (see **186** and **209**). This tense is commonly seen in action in reported speech *when the speaker's point of primary concern is moved back into the past.* See what happens in such circumstances to the example given in paragraphs **224** to **231**:

(224) *I said tomorrow would be my birthday. I said I should be fifty-one. I told you I would be obeyed, and you should obey me.*

(228) *I said I'd* (or *I would* or *should*) *probably be home late.*
I said you would be glad to hear . . .
Experience proved that where there was most confidence, there would be most freedom.

(229) *We believed we would find a cure for cancer if . . .* (This is *certain future* transferred to the past.)

(230) *I asked you if you would have some more tea?* (I asked you if you wanted it in the past.)

(231) *I told you I should arrive next* (or the following) *Monday.**
I asked if I should open the window, if we should go, if the waiter should serve coffee.
We were determined they should not pass.

236.   In the examples in **235**, *will* was automatically changed into *would,* and *shall* into *should;* and this is what normally happens in

* See **189**.

indirect speech. However, ambiguities may result from this automatic change. Transferred to the past, the example taken from **229** could be construed as being in the Conditional Mood (see **238**): to avoid this ambiguity, one might say *We believed a cure for cancer was assured if* . . . On the other hand, *I asked If I should open the window, if we should go,* could mean *I asked if I ought to open it, if we ought to go* (see **242**); and to avoid this, one could say *I asked if you wanted me to open the window, if you were ready to go.*

237. *He 'WOULD sit there* (**209,** *b*) expresses wilfulness; *he wouldn't move,* refusal. But beware of using *would* as a substitute for *wanted to* or *intended to.*

238. *Would and should* are also used to make up the *Conditional Mood.* Here we are not concerned with the speaker's point of view in or towards the natural order of events (see **156**), but with what he imagines as the consequence of an act desired or supposed (see **202,** *a* and *b*); thus:

    (*a*) *If we left now, we should arrive in good time.*
    (*b*) *Even if I knew, I wouldn't tell you.*
    (*c*) *If I did smoke, I would smoke a pipe.*
    (*d*) *I believe we should find a cure for cancer, provided we had the facilities for research.*

239. In the examples in **238,** the verb in the subordinate clause (beginning with *if*) could be considered as unmarked (cf. *We'll go out if it's fine,* **182**) and, for this reason, it is not expressed in the *Conditional Mood.* However, the Conditional can be used in a subordinate clause to suggest that the desired or supposed event might be fulfilled, e.g.

    (*a*) *If you would be interested* (there is a chance that you will be), *I should be very glad to send you a copy of my book.* Compare this with (*b*) *If you were* (and you are not), *you would do something about it.*

240. The *Conditional* is often used, in contrast with the Future Tense, as a mark of courtesy, deference or hesitation, to avoid a blunt or definite assertion. Compare *You will be glad to hear* . . . (I am boldly assuming you will) with the less assertive *You would be glad* . . . Similarly, *Would you have some more tea?* is more deferential than *Will you* . . .*?*; and *I should be grateful if you would reply urgently* is less imperative than *I shall be grateful if you will* . . .

241. Both in the Future-in-the-Past and in the Conditional, the choice between *would* and *should* depends on factors similar to those that decide the use of *will* and *shall*. As in **224**, there is a 'rule' which demands *I, and we, should* but *you, he, she, it and they, would*. This 'rule' is often applied to examples such as the one in **239** (*a*) to avoid two *woulds* or two *shoulds*, with different subjects, in one sentence. At the same time one finds a tendency for *would*, like *will*, to be used as an unmarked form for all persons, and for *should*, like *shall*, to mark something subjective in the speaker's attitude. As with *I'll*, there is in fluent speech a neutral *I'd*, which in an emphatic or exposed position could become either *I would* or *I should*.*

242. Apart from the subjective attitudes discussed in **231** and applying to *should* in both the Future-in-the-Past and the Conditional, obligation and expectation (**249**) can be expressed by *should*:

(*a*) *If the house caught fire, I know what I* **should** *do* (obligation), *but I'm not sure what I* **would** *do* (Conditional).

(*b*) *If you left at ten, you should arrive in time* (reasonable expectation). *If you left at nine, you certainly would.*

In these examples, *should* could not be replaced by *would*. In (*a*), *should* could replace *would* (see 'rule' in **241**) but the more positive *would* is necessary for the contrast, as it is in (*b*). Note that the *should* of obligation is not weakened to '*d* in fluent speech; *We'd go* (Conditional) *if we had the chance* but *I think we should go* (obligation).

243. *Should* also marks a higher degree of supposition in a case such as that exemplified in **239** (*a*); thus:

(*a*) *If, by any chance, you should be interested, I would be glad to send you a copy of my book;* or

(*b*) *Should you be interested by any chance, I would be* . . .

In (*b*), the *should*, strongly marked, cannot be replaced by *would*. It could be so replaced in (*a*), but if it were the emphasis on supposition would be lost unless the speaker stressed the word *if* or the phrase *by any chance*. Notice that in order to mark the *should* in *if you should be interested* and to avoid a second marking in the sentence, I used *would* in the second part of both (*a*) and (*b*), there having a choice.

* Radio broadcasters, writing *I'd* in their scripts, which are usually composed in colloquial style, are sometimes asked to revise their manuscripts for publication. They then find it hard to decide whether *I'd* should be written *I would* or *I should*.

244. *Should* cannot be replaced by *would* in examples such as:
(*a*) *I began this talk not intending that it should have an autobiographical element* (Somerset Maugham).
(*b*) *It is perhaps appropriate that I should be discussing this subject* (E. M. Forster).

Would have, should have

245. *Would have* (*done*), *should have* (*done*) are used
(*a*) when the Future Perfect is transferred to a point of view in past time: thus *I'll have finished this by Friday* becomes (*I said*) *I'd have finished it by Friday*: and
(*b*) as a Conditional-in-the-Past; e.g. *I did not go out last night. If I had* (*gone out*), *I would not have finished my essay.*

246. *Should have* is also used to suggest past obligation unfulfilled; e.g.
We should go now. In fact, we should have left an hour ago. In other words: *We have not gone yet but are obliged to go. In fact, we were obliged to leave an hour ago, but did not.* The obligation could remain unfulfilled because we were free to avoid it.

Sequence of Tenses in Conditional Sentences

247. In sentences composed of clauses beginning with *if* and of verbal constructions containing *will, shall, would* and *should*, certain combinations of tenses become stereotyped; e.g.

(*a*) *If it rains, the meeting will be cancelled.* (**182,** *b*)
(*b*) *I told you that if it rained the meeting would be cancelled.* (**235**)
(*c*) *I don't know the answer. If I did, I wouldn't tell you.* (**202, 238**)
(*d*) *I should be grateful if you would reply urgently.* (**240**)
(*e*) (*I didn't know.*) *If I had known, I would have told you.* (**245,** *b*)

248. The patterns in **247** are common, relating to common situations. But any other combination of tenses is possible if the meaning requires it; e.g.
(*a*) *I will certainly come to the meeting, if that will help.* (**182,** *d*)
(*b*) *You said you were waiting at the station. If you were there* (we assume the event was fulfilled), *somebody would surely have seen you.*
(*c*) *If it rained* (i.e. on the occasions when it did rain), *we would* (**237**) *stay indoors and read.*

Should, ought to, must, have to, am to

249. These words primarily express different degrees of obligation with regard to the unfulfilled event. *Ought to* is generally felt to express a stronger sense of obligation than *should*; and it often replaces *should* when a more resounding word is felt to be necessary. In very many usages the two expressions are interchangeable without any effect on the meaning. Both suggest (*a*) that the person or thing concerned has not taken certain action, is advised, required or expected to take it, but is still free to avoid it; or (*b*) that an event is expected but is not inevitable; e.g. (*a*) *We should, or ought to, go now* (but we might be tempted to stay), and (*b*) *It should, or ought to, be a fine day tomorrow* (but might not be). However, the following subtle distinction is sometimes discernible: *I should do this* tends to draw attention to what is advisable, required or expected for the future; *I ought to do it*, to what has been left undone. This distinction might occur in examples such as:

(*a*) *Applications should reach this office by January 1st* (that is required), and

(*b*) *You ought to apply without further delay.* (You haven't applied yet.)

250. (*a*) *Must* differs from *should* and *ought to* in that the person or thing concerned is *not* considered free to avoid the required or expected action. With *must*, action is imagined as inevitable.

(*b*) Note the special use of *must* in *You must be tired*, i.e. you cannot fail to be tired as a result of the activity in which you have been engaged. Here, neither obligation nor non-fulfilment is implied, but *must* serves to make a statement emphatically and to exclude the possibility of the contrary being true, so that the idea of inevitability is still present. (Note: *it can't be true*, **260,** *i*.) However, *must* is often used in this way when the speaker merely hopes or supposes that the contrary cannot be true.

251. *Have to* conveys the same idea as *must* in **250** (*a*) but—in the Present Tense at least—with a less compelling tone. *Have to*, spoken with a forceful stress, could express as much obligation as *must*, though it lacks in curtness of command. However, *must* is a defective verb and its missing parts are supplied by the parts of *have to*, as will be seen in **255**.

252. The past equivalent of *must*, in a marked position, is *had to*, though in an unmarked, subordinate position it remains *must*. Note

119

(*a*) *I must be very frank with you.* (Present.)

(*b*) *I had to be very frank with him.* (Past: not *must*, which could be mistaken for the Present.) But one could say *I felt I must be frank with him*, because here the principal verb, *felt*, makes it clear that one is thinking of the past.

(*c*) '*We must all hang together or we shall hang separately.*' (Present.)

(*d*) *It was Benjamin Franklin who said we must all hang together or we should all hang separately.* The tense of *was* and *said* show that the **SPPC** is in the past. Note that we could also say, *It was Franklin who said that we all had to hang together*: here emphasis is placed on past obligation.

253.   The opposite of *I must go* (i.e. of *I am obliged to go*) is *I must not go* (i.e. I am forbidden to go); but the negative is *I need not go* (i.e. I am not obliged to go). In *I must not go*, I am required NOT TO GO; in *I need not go*, I am not required to go at all if I do not want to. See also **273**.

254.   *I am to* (*do something*) means that I am obliged and bound to do it by some circumstance outside myself—by a plan, agreement, time-table, instruction, or something similar, which I am not considered free to ignore.

255.   The following table shows how the idea of *obligation without the option of avoiding it* is expressed in the various tenses:

Tense	Affirmative	Opposite	Negative
Present	(i) I am obliged to (go)	am forbidden to	am not obliged to
	(ii) I must (go)	must not	need not
	(iii) I have to (go)	— (1)	do not have to
	(iv) I am to (go)	am not to	—
Pre-Present	(i) I have been obliged to	have been forbidden to	have not been obliged to
	(ii) —	—	—
	(iii) have had to	—	have not had to
	(iv) —	—	—

Past	(i)	I was obliged to	was forbidden to	was not obliged to
	(ii)	must (unmarked)	must not (unmarked)	need not (unmarked)
	(iii)	had to (marked)	—	did not have to (marked)
	(iv)	was to (2)	was not to (marked)	—
Pre-Past	(i)	had been obliged to	had been forbidden to	had not been obliged to
	(ii)	—	—	—
	(iii)	had had to	—	had not had to
	(iv)	was to have (gone) (3)	—	—
Future	(i)	will be obliged to	will be forbidden to	will not be obliged to
	(ii)	must (unmarked)	must not	need not (unmarked) will not need to (marked)
	(iii)	will have to (marked)	—	will not have to (marked)
	(iv)	am to (4)	am not to	—

Notes

1. A blank in the table indicates that the corresponding form is not used in that position.
2. *I was to go to London* = that was the plan, those were my instructions.
3. *I was to have gone* = It had been planned that I should go, but I had not gone.
4. The plan (see **254**) covers the future.

Ought to have (been), must have (been)

256.   *Ought to have* (*been*) is a past equivalent of *ought to* (*be*), just as *should have* (*been*) is of *should* (*be*)—**246,** and suggests unfulfilled obligation; e.g.:

(Present) *Where is John? He ought to be home by now.*
(Past)   *Yes, he ought to have been home an hour ago.*

257.   *Must have been* is a past equivalent of *must* in the sense in which it is used in **250** (*b*):

(*a*)   *You walked all the way? You must have been tired at the end of it.*

(*b*)   *You did all that yesterday? You must have worked fast.*

The non-fulfilment of the obligation in **250** (*a*) is impossible because the obligation was inevitable—it *had* to be fulfilled.

Can, could, may, might

258.   These words express an opposite attitude to that of the previous group, in so far as they suggest *freedom* to act, or what is possible rather than what is required. Freedom to act, or possibility, may depend on:

(*a*) ability or power in the actor (person or thing);

(*b*) lack of opposition;

(*c*) positive permission;

(*d*) what is probable, what circumstances permit, or what happens by chance.

259.   Undoubted freedom to take a definite line of action is normally expressed in the present tense by *can*, whatever that freedom may depend on. *Can* is the normal, unmarked member of the pair *can v may*. In its strong unmarked form, *can* is specially concerned with **258**, *a* and *b*. *May* is the marked form specially concerned with **258**, *c* and *d*. Thus:

Unmarked	*Marked*
1. (weak) CAN	MAY (permission, chance, external circumstances)

2. (strong) CAN (ability,
    internal power, lack of
    opposition)	

At the same time, while *can* suggests freedom to take a definite line of action, *may* suggests freedom to take one (or more) of two (or more) *alternatives*, when exactly which line of action will be taken is uncertain.

260.   There are therefore times when *can* and *may* are interchangeable without noticeable effect on meaning; other times when they

are not interchangeable, or when a careful writer has some subtle distinction in mind in making a deliberate choice. Examples:

(*a*) *I can drive much better now* (ability: not *may*).

(*b*) *I **may** drive much better now but I'm still nervous* (I admit that it is possible: in that sense, not *can*).

(*c*) *Can I borrow your pen?* (*can* unmarked, weak. The marked *may*, which asks specifically for permission in such a case, is for that reason felt to be more considerate: it is also held to be more 'correct', though *can I* is commonly used).

(*d*) *You **can** (borrow my pen), but you may not* (the standard pedantic reply to (*c*)).

(*e*) *What will happen on Tuesday? Anything can happen* (unmarked, weak) or *Anything may happen* (which of the alternatives will be taken is uncertain). *Will the Government be defeated? That can happen* (that line of action is definitely open) or *That may happen* (that is one of the possibilities).

(*f*) *You may lead a horse to water but you can't make it drink.* (*You can lead* would also be acceptable in this case and might come more naturally to many English speakers: the emphasis is not on that part of the proverb and it would be natural to use the weak, unmarked form there. However, *may* at the beginning of the proverb provides a contrast with the main point, *can't*, for which there is no option, since the point is that you *haven't the power* to make the horse drink. We *could* say *you may not make it drink* but that would suggest either that you will not have permission or that it is probable you will not succeed.)

(*g*) *He can be very amusing* (he has the ability) *but last night he was dull. You never know what he will be like: he may be amusing, he may have nothing to say* (either is a possibility). *He may be amusing but I don't like his jokes* (I admit that is possible, but . . .)

(*h*) *Don't wait for me, I may be late* (or I may not be—either is possible). *Now I'm the boss I can be late if I want to be* (that line is open to me, I have the power).

(*i*) *Can this be true? No, it can't be.* (Is that specific course open? No, that specific course is not.) *It can be true* (that specific course *is* open) or *It may be true* (or it may not be—either is a possibility). (Note: *It must be true*, **250**, *b*.)

261.   *Can* frequently precedes certain verbs of perception, e.g. *I can see a ship. Can you hear me? I can remember exactly what happened.* In such examples, the meaning is almost identical with that of *I see. Do you hear? I remember.* However, in *I can see*, etc., we are more concerned with the freedom to perform the act; in *I see*, with the act

fulfilled. This distinction appears more clearly in the past tense: *We had a marvellous view from here yesterday—we could see for miles* but *Have you seen my watch anywhere? Yes, I saw it on your dressing-table.* (See also **266.**)

262.   *Could* and *might* are:

(*a*) past equivalents of *can* and *may* (but see **263** and **271**); and
(*b*) less definite expressions of the ideas conveyed by *can* and *may*.

263.   In the past, *I can speak* (*English fairly well*) becomes *I could speak* (*it fairly well a few years ago*); and the examples in **260**, transferred to past reported speech, would become *I asked you if I could borrow your pen, I said you could but you might not, He warned us that anything could happen, anything might happen*, etc. However, the same sort of ambiguity is likely to arise here as we found when *will* and *shall* were put into the past (**236**). *Could*, as we shall see below, has other functions; and it is becoming rare for *might* to be used with the idea of permission in the past. *You might not use my pen* is much less likely to suggest '*you did not have permission to use it*' than '*it is, or was, possible that you would not use it*'. Thus to turn **260** (*d*) into the past without ambiguity, one would have to say *I said you could but I didn't say you may* or *I didn't give you permission* (*to do so*).

264.   Examples of *could* and *might* as less definite versions of *can* and *may* are:

(*a*) *I can be there by six* (definite). *I could be there by six* (less definite, more hesitant, a tentative suggestion).
(*b*) *Could I borrow your pen?* (more deferential and polite than *can I?*).
(*c*) *Might I borrow it?* (politer still).
(*d*) *Electric irons could be dangerous: they might give you a severe shock* (less positive than *can be, may give*).

In (*d*), *might* serves to give warning of a possibility that is undesirable. Spoken with stress and a particular intonation, it could indicate (perhaps with pleading or impatience) a desirable possibility; e.g. *You might tell me what he said* (I wish you would tell me—you are unkind, or annoying, not to tell me).

265.   Furthermore, *could* and *might* could be substituted for *would*, (*should*) in the pattern of conditional sentences:

(*a*) *Can you climb that tree? I could if I tried.*
(*b*) *Be careful. If you slipped here, you might kill yourself.*

(c) 'We might consider trade sanctions if we thought they would be effective' (a London newspaper).

266. A very common mistake by foreign students is due to failure to realise that *could*, like other modal verbs, expresses an attitude towards the act *unfulfilled*: it does not convey the idea that the act has been accomplished. Thus, *I could pass my examination* tells us something about my ability, not my accomplishment. A natural reaction of the native-English speaker to the statement *I could pass my examination* would be *I'm sure you* **could**, *but* **did** *you (pass)?* To give the impression that the act was accomplished in spite of the demands it made on my limited ability and energy, I would have to say *I was able*, or *I managed, to pass my examination* or *I succeeded in passing it*. Nevertheless, the idea of fulfilment is sometimes included in *could* in questions and the negative; e.g. *The police tried to capture this famous outlaw. Could they capture him?* (meaning *did they?*) *No, they could not* (from which we imply *they did not*). *They could have done* (see **268,** c), *but they only managed to capture his horse*.

Can have, could have, may have, might have

267. *Where's Robert? Where can he have gone? He can't have gone far. Oh yes, he can have gone anywhere*, i.e. where has he been able to go, or where is it (definitely) possible that he has gone? He has not been able to go far, or surely it is not possible that he has gone far. It is quite possible he has gone anywhere.

268. *I could have (gone)* might be:

(a) a past or more hesitant equivalent of the usage quoted in **267,** e.g. *Where could Robert have gone?* i.e. Where is (or was) it possible that he went (or had gone). Another common example would be *I heard you go out. But you couldn't have done*, i.e. it was not possible for you to hear me;

(b) an example of the Past Conditional, e.g. *Could you climb that tree when you were a boy?—I could have done if I had been allowed to* (cf. *would have*, **245,** b);

(c) an indication that the ability to fulfil the act was present but that the act itself was not accomplished. Examples: *I could have passed my examination easily but I made too many stupid mistakes* and *When I saw the results I could have wept*, i.e. I felt like weeping (but did not weep).

269. *May have (gone)* is of wider currency than *can have (gone)* and

applies the idea of possibility (but not of permission) to the prelude to the present or to definite past:

(*a*) *You may have noticed many examples of this kind* (it is possible that you have noticed);

(*b*) *When you were in London, you may have noticed . . .* (it is possible that you noticed . . .)

270. *Might have* (*gone*) can be

(*a*) a past or more hesitant equivalent of the usages in **269**. *You might have noticed* could mean either 'it was possible that you noticed (or had noticed)', or 'it is rather vaguely possible that you have noticed (noticed, or had noticed)';

(*b*) an example of the Past Conditional, e.g. *I might have won a prize if I had worked harder*;

(*c*) an indication that a line of action, together with alternatives, was open, but was not taken: *Life is full of stories of what might have been.* As in **264**, the line of action, not taken, was desirable (*You might have told me*, i.e. I wish you had done so) or undesirable (*You might have been killed*); in these two examples the pattern of stress and intonation are quite distinct.

271. The use of *can, could, may* and *might* in the principal tenses might be summarised thus:

POSSIBILITY

Tense	Ability	Permission	Probability
Present	(i) I am able to see	I am allowed to see	It is possible that I see, i.e. perhaps I see
	(ii) I can (1) see	I can, or MAY, (2) see	I MAY (3) see
Pre-Present	(i) I have been able to see (4)	I have been allowed to see	It is possible that I have seen
	(ii) —	—	I MAY have seen
Past	(i) I was able to see (4)	I was allowed to see	It is, or was, possible that I saw
	(ii) I could see, (5) I could have seen, (6)	I could (or, rarely, might) see	I may, or might, have seen

Pre-Past	(i) I had been able to see (4)	I had been allowed to see	It is, or was, possible that I had seen
	(ii) I could have seen (6)	—	I may, or might, have seen
Future	(i) I will be able to see	I will be allowed to see	It is possible that I will see
	(ii) I can see	I can, or MAY, see	I MAY see
Condit-ional	(i) I would be able to see	I would be allowed to see	It is possible that I would see
	(ii) I could see	I could, or MIGHT, see	I MIGHT see
Past Condit-ional	(i) I would have been able to see	I would have been allowed to see	It is possible that I would have seen
	(ii) I could have seen	I could have (or, rarely, might have) seen	I MIGHT have seen

Notes

1. *I can see* makes a positive statement about my present ability. In a hesitant or tentative expression (see **264,** *a*), *could* can be used even in the present tense.

2. *May*, in this column, emphasises the idea of permission. *Might* marks the idea more tentatively, especially when permission is asked (**264,** *c*).

3. *May* (probability) and *might* (tentative or past) suggest alternatives, e.g. *I may go* can mean *Perhaps I will go, perhaps I will not, perhaps I will do something else.* On the other hand, *can* expresses possibility without this element of uncertainty as to which course will be taken.

4. In the tenses referring to action before now (Pre-present, Past, Pre-past), *able to* suggests fulfilment as well as ability.

5. In contrast to 4, *could* suggests ability but not necessarily fulfilment. *I could pass—and either did pass or did not.*

6. *I could have seen*, i.e. I could see but did not (Past) or I had had the opportunity but had not taken it (Pre-past).

Sequence of Tenses with can, may, could might

272. The choice between *can* and *could* and between *may* and *might* may also (**247**) be decided by stereotyped combinations of tenses. See what happens when *can, may*, etc., are applied to the examples in **247** and **248**:

    247.   (*a*) *If it rains, the meeting can* (or *may*) *be cancelled.*
            (*b*) *If it rained, the meeting could* (or *might*) *be cancelled.*
            (*c*) *If I did* (*know the answer*), *I couldn't* (*mightn't*) *tell you.*
            (*d*) *I should be glad if you could.*
            (*e*) *If I had known, I could have* (*might have*) *told you.*

    248.   (*a*) *I can come if that will help. I could come if that would help.*
            (*b*) *If you were there, somebody could have* (*might have*) *helped you.*
            (*c*) *If it rained, we could* (*might*) *stay indoors.*

Need

273. *Need* is sometimes used as modal verb, i.e. to express an attitude towards unfulfilled activity (e.g. *you needn't go*, **253**), sometimes not (e.g. *Do you need this piece of paper?*). As a non-modal verb, it follows the patterns *Do you need* (*it*)? *No, I don't. He needs it.* As a modal verb, it can follow either (*a*) *will, would*, etc., in the interrogative, negative and third person singular of the affirmative, or (*b*) the ordinary 'full' verbs, thus: (*a*) *Need we tell him? We need not tell him. He need never know*, or (*b*) *Do you need to make that noise? You don't need to. In any case, your father needs to be quiet.* In the examples just given there appears to be a distinction between *Need we tell him?* which suggests the idea of *Surely we are not obliged to tell him?* (cf. **253**) and *Do you need to make that noise?* suggesting *Is that necessary?* In any case, sleep is necessary for Father. A similar distinction is noticeable in *You need not stay* (you may go) and *You don't need to stay* (it isn't necessary, there's nothing you can do). Similarly, *We didn't need to stay* suggests that staying was unnecessary; thus we were free to stay or go as we pleased. On the other hand, *We needn't have stayed* implies that we have stayed, or we stayed, unnecessarily.

274.   *Dare* is likewise both an ordinary, non-modal verb (*dare all things, I dare you to dive from here*) and a modal verb. As a modal verb it can follow both of the patterns referred to in **273**: thus *Dare you do it? You dare not do it. Dare he do it?* or *Do I dare (to)* eat a peach? I did not dare (to)* look. Who dares (to)* stop me?*

* *to* generally optional.

CHAPTER TEN

Infinitive versus -ing

275. The problems here are to know

(*a*) whether to use the infinitive without *to* (*I must go*) or the infinite with *to* (*I want to go*); and

(*b*) whether to use the infinitive (*I refuse to go, prefer to go*) or the verb-form ending in -*ing* (*I enjoy going, prefer going*).

276. These are largely questions of plain facts: the student must become familiar—through hearing or reading the language or through drill—with a variety of patterns and constructions in which the infinitive or the -*ing* form is used. Some of the commonest of these patterns are given in paragraphs **284** to **300**. However, a distinction in aspect, similar to that marking the difference between *I go* and *I am going* (Chapter Seven), is also noticeable in *infinitive v -ing*.

277. While the infinitive and the -*ing* form serve a variety of purposes, the contrast in *infinitive v -ing* seems in current English to be basically a question of *act in general, or a specific act v process in which the actor is engaged*. This might be expressed:

Unmarked	Marked
1. SEE (weak: the act in general)	SEEING (process in which one is engaged)
2. SEE (strong: a specific act, a fresh act in the course of events)	

These distinctions are noticeable in the following examples:

(*a*) Unmarked, weak: *I like to see children happy.*

(*b*) Unmarked, strong: *Excuse me, I would like to see your passport.*

(*c*) *Don't draw the curtains—I like seeing the view.*

278.   The distinction between the unmarked *see* and the marked
seeing might be illustrated by diagrams similar to those in **137.**

SEE

FIG. 30
(cf. Fig. 12)

FIG. 31
(cf. Fig. 13)

The strong *see* could be shown thus:

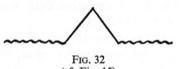

FIG. 32
(cf. Fig. 15)

the jump of the electric needle marking a fresh act in the course of
events.

279.   The distinction illustrated above is noticeable in many stereotyped expressions where either the infinitive or the *-ing* form *must*
be used (e.g. *I refuse to go, I enjoy dancing*), as well as in constructions where both *may* be used (e.g. *I prefer to walk, I prefer walking*).
The student can tell only from experience when he is free to use both
forms. Sometimes the speaker may be faced with what appears to be
a completely 'free variant'; for example, he could say *they began to
run* or *they began running* without any apparent distinction in meaning at all. In this instance a precise distinction in meaning, similar to
that illustrated in **278,** might be made: *began to run* could stress the
start of a fresh act, the first strides forward; while *begin running*
could draw attention to the initiation of the process, of the continuous movement. The chances are, however, that most users of English
would choose *to run* or *running* in these cases by accident, or for the
sake of euphony, rhythm or variety.

280.   While both the infinitive and the *-ing* express aspects of
activity, and in form are parts of what is traditionally called a verb,
the verbal element often seems to be stronger in the infinitive. *I like*

131

to see suggests that I want to perform *that act*. In the *-ing*, there is generally either a noun element or an adjectival element. The *noun* element stresses the *process* in which someone or something is engaged; the *adjectival* element describes how the person or thing is *engaged*. Thus:

(NOUN) *Walking is good for you.* (Cf. *Exercise is good for you.*) *Yes, but I don't like walking—it makes me too hot. Don't speak about walking to me.*

(ADJECTIVE) *Walking home the other evening, I was nearly run over by a taxi: I saw the taxi coming straight at me. So-and-so has an extraordinary knowledge of English— he's a walking dictionary.*

281. Usages will be found where the distinction in **277** and **278** does not seem to apply. Examples:

(*a*) *Jumping into his car, he raced off in pursuit.* Here we are concerned with two consecutive acts—he jumped, then he raced. Compare this example with:

(*b*) *Racing to his car, he jumped in and drove off in pursuit*, where the act *raced* precedes the act *jumped*. In both examples we have a contrasting pair, *-ing* form *v* finite verb. The effect of this contrast is to place the action expressed by the *-ing* form in a subordinate position, and to throw the spot-light on to the action expressed by the finite verb. This contrast is often used as a formal, stylistic device, especially in journalistic writing, to reduce the number of finite verbs in a sentence. Note, however, that in

(*c*) *Ignoring the traffic lights, he raced off in pursuit*, *ignoring* refers to a process in which the driver is engaged as he goes along, as well as expressing an action which is formally subordinated to *raced*. The actions here are not consecutive, as they are in (*a*) and (*b*), but are simultaneous, and the phrase *ignoring the traffic lights* could either precede or follow the main part of the sentence.

282. The infinitive itself can have both a neutral or completed aspect, as in *We ought to go*, and an uncompleted aspect, as in *We ought to be going*. In these two examples, *to go* is either the weak, unmarked form, or it expresses finality; *to be going* marks the process of taking one's leave, or of being on one's way. The uncompleted aspect of the infinitive is also commonly found after *will, would, shall, should, must, could, may, might, had better, had rather, had sooner, want, seem, appear, happen*, etc.

132

283. The infinitive can also have a 'Perfect' form, e.g. *to have gone* expressing the idea of *prelude to the present* (see **161**) or of *prelude to the past*. Thus:

(a) *I am glad* (now) *to see you are better* (now); BUT *I am glad to have met you* (in time ending at the point NOW), and *I would like* (now) *to have seen that play* (before now).

(b) *I was glad* (then) *to see it* (then); *If I had been there* (unreal past), *I would have done my best* (imagined consequence in the past) *to stop it*. BUT *I was glad* (then) *to have seen it* (before then).

(c) Note that one can say either *I meant* (then) *to tell you all about it* (then), or *I meant* (in the past) *to have told you* (before now). In the latter example, the speaker's point of primary concern shifts from past time when his intention was formed or held, to the present, until when his intention has not yet been fulfilled. A similar shift is noticeable in *I was to have seen him*.

Infinitive without *to*

284. The infinitive without *to* follows:

(a) *do*, emphatic, negative and interrogative, as in **221**: *Please do come if you can. Don't go. What did you say?*

(b) *will, would, shall, should, must, can, could, may, might* (see the many examples in Chapter Nine).

(c) *dare* and *need* in the negative and interrogative, when they are used without *do*. E.g. *I dare not go. Dare I go? I need not go. Need I go?* But *I don't dare (to) go. Do I dare (to) go? I don't need to go. Do I need to go?*

(d) *had better, had rather, had sooner*. E.g. *We'd better go now. I'd rather die. I'd sooner go for a bathe.*

(e) *let, make*. E.g. *Please let me know. What makes you think that?* But note the passive: *Shall I be allowed to say a few words? Yes, but you'll be made to sit down again after five minutes.*

(f) *help*, as in *please help me lift this trunk*. However, *to* can also be used after *help*, especially in a more complicated sentence; e.g. *Volunteer workers helped the farmers to gather in the harvest.*

(g) *see, watch, hear, feel, notice*, and words fulfilling a similar function, as in *I saw him stop, watched him enter the building, heard him come out again, felt him brush past me, noticed him hesitate*. The same construction applies to *know* in its perfect and past tenses: *I have known him go without food for days on end. I had never known him lose his temper before. I never knew him make a bad mistake.* But

133

note the passive: *He was seen to stop, was never known to lose his temper*; and see **295**.

Infinitive with *to*

285. The infinitive with *to* follows:

(*a*) *have, ought, used* (as in **175**), and the various parts of *be*, as in *We have (ought, used, are) to go*.

(*b*) *do not need* (cf. **284, c**).

(*c*) *come, get*, in *come to realise, get to like somebody* (see *prelude to the act*, **213**).

286. Other common occurrences of the infinitive with *to* are:

(*a*) to indicate purpose; e.g. *We got up to go. I have just returned to live in England. We arrived at the station early (in order) to get a good seat on the train.*

(*b*) after certain verbs; e.g. *agree, appear, decide, endeavour, fail, happen, hesitate, manage, promise, refuse, seem, take care, try, undertake, want*. Thus *I want (promise, manage, etc.) to go*.

(*c*) after certain verbs followed by a direct object; e.g. *advise, allow, ask, cause, encourage, expect, force, persuade, prefer, teach, want*. Thus *I advise (allow, etc.) you to go*.

(*d*) after certain adjectives; e.g. *able, delighted, glad, happy, likely, pleased, sorry, sure*. Thus *I am able (glad, etc.) to go*.

-ing

287. The *-ing* form follows:

(*a*) certain verbs which are obviously concerned with a continuing action or process; e.g. *keep (on) writing, go on writing*.

(*b*) certain verbs which look *back* on the process; e.g. *stop writing, finish writing, give up working, remember seeing*.

(*c*) other verbs which throw emphasis on the process; e.g. *enjoy swimming. Do you mind waiting a few minutes? I am used to waiting. I can't help laughing* (i.e. *I can't stop, or prevent myself from, laughing*). Note that *avoid* fits into this pattern: *one can't avoid making mistakes*.

(*d*) all prepositions, except the *to* of the infinitive; e.g. *Let's talk about fishing. He earns his living by translating. Before or after eating. Kindly refrain from smoking. Succeed in climbing. Suspected of cheating, fond of reading, tired of standing, weary of being continually*

criticised. Instead of criticising, do something to help. I don't object to waiting. I can't advise you without knowing the facts.
   Note (*e*): *Is this book worth reading?*

288. The *-ing* form commonly occurs as a participle, as in the examples in **281,** either to describe the person or thing to which it relates, or as a means of subordinating one action to another, or as a stylistic device to avoid a finite verb. Further examples are:

   (*a*) *Running downstairs, he tripped and fell heavily.* Here, *running* relates to, and describes, the person who tripped. At the same time, *running* is subordinated to *tripped* and *fell.* As all the actions are more or less simultaneous, the participle phrase could also come after *fell heavily*, in which case it would stress the cause of the fall.

   (*b*) *We sat and watched the moon rising over the lake.* Here, *rising* relates to and describes the moon, not the people who sat and watched it. In this case, if the participial phrase began the sentence, *rising* might be felt to refer to the watchers, and that would hardly make sense unless they were seated in an aircraft.

   (*c*) *Arriving an hour late because of fog, the delegates were driven straight to the conference hall* (quotation from a newspaper). *Arriving* relates to the delegates, is subordinated to *were driven*, and allows the spot-light of emphasis to be directed on to one finite verb.

289. Other common uses of the *-ing* form are—

   (*a*) as an adjective preceding the noun described; e.g. *The boy stood on the burning deck. An interesting story. A tiring day. A drowning man. The sinking ship.* While every full verb could end in *-ing* and could potentially be used as an adjective in this way, only certain ones have been regularly adopted as adjectives, and of these only a few are capable of comparison. We can say *more interesting, most interesting, more tiring, most tiring,* but not **more drowning, *more sinking.* Moreover, to be used in this way, the *-ing* form must be really descriptive—it is not sufficient that it should refer to an action in progress. Thus *the reading public* describes and specifies a section of the public, which may not be actually reading at the time; but we do not say **the reading boy* merely to indicate *the boy who is reading.* Note that in *the 'burning 'deck, the 'reading 'public,* stress falls equally on the adjective-word and the noun, and intonation remains more or less level.

   (*b*) as an adjunct indicating the purpose which something serves; thus *a 'reading-lamp* is a lamp for reading by, *a 'drawing-pin* is a pin used for fastening a drawing to a board, *a 'swimming-pool* is a pool to swim in, and so on. Note that in these cases the stress is on the adjunct, and intonation drops with the noun.

Cases in which the speaker has a choice between infinitive and -ing form

290.   There are times when either the infinitive or the *-ing* form could acceptably fit into the sentence, but not with equal meaning. Examine the following pairs of sentences:

(*a*) *He stood by the gate to watch a train come in.*	*He stood there watching it come in.*
(*b*) *We arrived to find the ship had already left.*	*We arrived feeling exhausted.*
(*c*) *He went on to tell us this astonishing story.*	*He went on talking.*
(*d*) *We stopped to eat our lunch.*	*We stopped eating our lunch.*
(*e*) *Did you to remember to post my letter?* (Did you remember that I asked you to post it, and did you do it?)	*Do you remember taking a letter to the post last Thursday?* (You took it: do you remember that action?)
(*f*) *You were engaged to carry out research, not to decide policy.*	*Suppose you are engaged in carrying out an important piece of research.*

291.   In the left-hand column in **290,** *to watch, to find, to tell, to eat, to post, to carry out,* all indicate either a fresh act in the course of events and indicate the purpose or the consequence of *stood, arrived, went on,* etc. In the other column, *watching* tells us how *he* was occupied; *feeling exhausted* describes the people who arrived; *talking* indicates a process continuing; *eating,* a process ended; *taking a letter,* a process which went on last Thursday (cf. *You remember you took a letter,* which draws attention more to the completed act); and *carrying out* indicates the process in which you are spending your time.

292.   Sometimes there is a change of meaning in the word preceding the infinitive or *-ing* form; for example:

(*a*) *I can't help you solve this problem—it's too difficult.*	*I can't help* (i.e. prevent myself from) *solving this problem— it's too easy.*

(*b*) *You must try* (make an attempt) *to be more careful.* | *Try turning the handle the other way and see what happens* (make that test or experiment).

293. Obvious examples of the *-ing* form as a noun are found in the following pairs:

(*a*) *Do write to me please.* | *Does your child do writing at school yet?* (cf. *Does he do music?*)

(*b*) *I want to clean the car.* | *The car needs* (or *wants*) *cleaning.*

'Free' variants

294. As we saw in **279,** the speaker may be faced with apparently 'free' variants in association with certain words, e.g. *begin, start, continue. They began to run, began running, started to run, started running*, may all mean exactly the same, though individual users of the language might see or imagine some slight distinction between them; and *We shall continue to write our broadcasts in the English of excellent conversation* might be in no way different from *We shall continue writing*, etc. Yet even with these words it cannot be assumed that the speaker is free to use either the infinitive or the *-ing* form indiscriminately. One would rarely find a comparable alternative to *I begin to see, to wonder, to think, to believe*, no doubt for the reason suggested in **146;** nor an alternative to *Baby is just beginning to walk*, since *beginning walking* would raise the kind of objection discussed in the footnote to **11** (*b*).

295. Freedom of choice is generally possible with the words in **284** (*g*). Whether one says *I heard the 'phone ring* or *I heard it ringing* may be purely a matter of habit or imitation of someone else's speech. On the other hand, a distinction between a specific, completed act, and a continuous process might be seen in the following examples:

Specific, completed act	Continuing process
(*a*) *Did anyone actually see the car crash into the tree?*	*No, but this man saw the car behind it slowing down.*
(*b*) *And did you hear the policeman blow his whistle?*	*Yes, and I heard all the people shouting afterwards.*
(*c*) *We saw the boat sink.*	*We watched it sinking.*

(*d*) *I noticed him turn on a switch,*

(*e*) *and felt the whole floor shudder.*

(*f*) *He was seen to fall.*

I felt the floor rising, and noticed him gripping the lever hard.

Rocks were seen falling from the cliffs.

296. Similarly, with *prefer, intend*:

(*a*) *Can I offer you a lift? Thank you—I prefer to walk.*

I prefer walking in the evening— it's much cooler than at midday.

(*b*) *Where do you intend to hang this picture?*

Nowhere yet, I intend keeping it hidden till Mother's gone.

In preferring one thing *to* another—e.g. *I prefer walking to going in a crowded bus*—the *-ing* form saves the speaker from a tongue-twisting repetition of *to*, though *I prefer to walk than to go*, etc., would occur naturally in native-English speech.

297. After *like, love, hate*, it sometimes makes no difference which form the speaker uses, while at the other times the contrast observed in **277** is so obvious that he has no choice. Thus one can say either *I like (love, hate) to have my meals served that way* or *I like (love, hate) having*, etc. But in *Would you like to go to the concert this evening?* reference is made to one specific act, and *Would you like going?* would be unacceptable in that context. Take care not to jump to the conclusion that *would (should) like* always requires the infinitive; it can be followed by the *-ing* form if the speaker's concern is with the process rather than with a specific act; e.g. *I would like swimming if it were not for the mess it makes of my hair.*

298. Sometimes we have a contrast between an infinitive which points forward to a fresh act, and an *-ing* form which refers back to a process, as in *remember to post* and *remember posting*. In *It's a good idea to put another lock on the door, to put*—as I see it—refers to a specific act not yet accomplished; while in *It's a good idea putting another lock on*, etc., *putting* looks back to something that has been done. This particular contrast is noticeable in *Aren't you ashamed of appearing in public like that?* (the chances are that you have already appeared like it) and *Aren't you ashamed to appear like it?* (which might refer more to the general idea or to something about to happen). However, in these examples, such a contrast—when it is

made—would need to be reinforced by intonation, and might well be made more by intonation than by choice of infinitive or *-ing*.

299. With *ashamed* (see **298**) the infinitive requires *to*; the *-ing* form, *of*. Note the change of preposition in:

(*a*) *I'm afraid to take any more aspirin—I've had three already.* *I'm afraid of taking aspirin—it always upsets me.*

(*b*) *It's a pleasure to welcome you here.* *When may we have the pleasure of welcoming you again?*

(*c*) *This is a good opportunity to improve your English.* *You must take every opportunity of improving your English.*

(*d*) *Let's make one more attempt to get to the top.* *All their attempts at reaching the summit failed.*

(*e*) *They decided (were determined) to try again.* *They decided (were determined) on pressing forward.*

In such cases, the choice between the infinitive and *-ing* may be made for the sake of clarity or variety. Thus in the sentence *They decided to make another attempt to cross the river, and to abandon their equipment*, we might change *to cross* to *at crossing*, either to make it clear that *to abandon* follows *decided*, not *attempt*, or to avoid three infinitives in succession.

300. For the subject of a sentence, modern English can have either the infinitive or an *-ing* form; e.g.:

(*a*) $\left\{ \begin{array}{l} \textit{To learn} \\ \textit{Learning} \end{array} \right.$ *a new language at fifty is no easy matter.*

The modern tendency in this situation, however, seems to be to prefer the *-ing* form, which is more noun-like (see **280**), though the infinitive is considered obligatory in established sayings such *To err is human*. In this pattern, *to* must be included with the infinitive; but note:

(*b*) *Speak frankly is something he could never do* (i.e. he could never speak frankly). Here the *-ing* form could not be used.

In sentences on the pattern *It's nice to get up in the morning, but nicer to stay in bed*, the infinitive is usually found, but the *-ing* form may occur if we are specially concerned with the process, e.g. *Don't hold your pen that way—it's easier holding it like this*. After *it's no good, it's no use*, the *-ing* form is general; e.g. *It's no use crying over spilt milk*. An infinitive or *-ing* form could begin a sentence without being the subject of it; e.g. *To speak* (or *Speaking*) *frankly, I think you're making a great mistake. To tell the truth,* often found at the beginning of a sentence, is a fixed expression with no alternative, but in this example there is a sense of purpose (**286,** *a*), as also in *To cut a long story short, he was never seen again.*

CHAPTER ELEVEN

Prepositions and
Adverbial Particles

Prepositions

301. The prepositions express relationships in space between one thing and another, and relationships in time between events. They might be considered basically as applications of the ideas contained in the scheme:

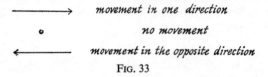

movement in one direction

no movement

movement in the opposite direction

FIG. 33

to something having no, or an unspecified, dimension; to something having one dimension; having two dimensions; or three dimensions. In space, let us call something with no, or unspecified dimension, a POINT; with one dimension, a LINE; two dimensions, a SURFACE, having area; three, a SPACE, having volume. (Be careful to distinguish between 'space (not time)' and 'a space, something having volume'.) In time we can imagine a point of time, or a period. In using the prepositions we are concerned not so much with objective measurements, i.e. with the actual dimensions of the things to which we are referring, as with how we imagine them to be at the time of speaking. Thus we can imagine a town as a point on the map, as a surface to go across, or as a space we live in or walk through. Moreover, a point itself, seen through a microscope, may appear to have area which can be covered or space which can be penetrated.

302. It is possible to fit a great number of usages into this scheme, and there is much to be said, in teaching the prepositions, for

beginning with those usages which fall into a scheme of this kind easily. On the other hand, many usages are very difficult to systematise. This is not surprising. Some of the relationships we want to express are very complex. We express them by little words whose full meaning could only be explained in long circumlocutions. Moreover, the number of these little words is limited, and each may have to serve a variety of purposes. Nevertheless, the use of prepositions in English can be remarkably, almost geometrically, precise, and the student would be well advised to be as clear about them as he can, without forcing natural usage into an artificial framework.

No, or unspecified, dimension

to, at, from

303. Movement in the direction of a point is expressed by TO; in the opposite direction, by FROM. Imagine two things, X and Y, occupying two different positions; and *imagine* the position of Y to be a point or to be of unspecified dimension. If X moves so as to occupy more or less the same position as Y, then we say that *X moves TO Y*. So X is now AT Y. If we now remove X, we take it FROM Y. Thus

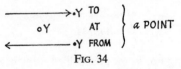

FIG. 34

Remember that *to* and *from* express movement; *at*, no movement. All three can be applied to a point both in space and in time: *This train goes from London to Edinburgh in six hours, stopping only at York. Your lesson is from nine to* (or *till*) *ten in the morning: it starts promptly at nine.* (But *Your lesson will last till ten*—not *to*, when *from* is omitted.)

304. Other examples of *to, at* and *from*:

TO. *Go to bed. Listen to me. Does this book belong to you? Best wishes to you all. I passed* (*my examination*), *thanks to you. Be kind to animals, don't be cruel to them. Stick to your principles.* The *to* of the infinitive frequently points *forward* (⟶) to a fresh act in the course of events: see particularly **286** (*a*) and **290**.

AT. *I live at this address, at number 30. At what time shall we meet? I'm busy at the moment.* Notice especially:

(*a*) the idea of stationary relationship with unspecified dimension in *I'm sitting at a desk, at a table, at the window* (contrast: *Your book is on,* or *in, the desk, on the table. Who stuck that paper on the window?*); *standing at the door* (cf. *a name painted on the door*);

(*b*) the same idea applied to a general concept (see **114**): *at work, at play, at rest, at fault, at peace, at war* (cf. *in the war,* to emphasise the period, and also to specify which war), *at sea* (cf. *on the sea,* i.e. on the surface, and *in the sea,* i.e. in the volume of water), *at night* (cf. *in the night,* to emphasise the period, and either to specify which night, or to distinguish night from day);

(*c*) concentration on the final point of the movement: *aim at, arrive at, laugh at, shoot at, throw at* (note: *throw the ball at me,* i.e. in my direction, *not AT me,* so as to hit me. Similarly, *point to the blackboard,* but *don't point at other people—it's rude*).

FROM. *How far is the bus stop from here? Let's escape from it all. Tell me the worst, don't hide it from me. No one can prevent me (from) finding out. To be absent from work. Refrain from spitting.*

towards, as far as

305. *To* envisages completed movement and suggests that X actually reaches Y, or will reach Y unless prevented. Movement in the direction of Y, without the idea of completion, is expressed by TOWARDS. This applies only to space, though we sometimes say *towards* (*six o'clock*) to mean *about or nearly then.* To emphasise the length of the journey to Y, which is eventually reached, we say *X goes AS FAR AS Y.*

till (or until), since

306. *As far as* is used only for space. To emphasise length of time, eventually concluded, we say TILL or UNTIL the final point. *If you want a walk, I'll come with you as far as the shops, but I am not ready yet—I shall be busy till five o'clock.* SINCE, as we saw in **161**, means 'in the progress of time from a specified point in the past until the speaker's point of primary concern', whether SPPC is present or past. E.g. *I have not seen him since Thursday. Yesterday was the hottest day since* 1925.

(away) from, near

307. *From* (with space) is reinforced by AWAY, which stresses the idea of the separation of the two positions held by X and Y. Thus *X is at Y. Now it moves AWAY from Y.* When X occupies a different position from Y, and is stationary, then we say

$$X \text{ is } \begin{cases} \textit{so many inches (miles, etc.)} \\ \textit{some distance, a long way} \\ \textit{not far} \end{cases} (\textit{away}) \textit{ from } Y.$$

If Y is mentioned, *from* must precede it, and *away* is optional; but see the section on Adverbial Particles. To emphasise the *shortness* of the distance between X and Y, we say *X is NEAR Y.*

for

308. To express the object or purpose of the *to* movement, or to indicate the person or thing affected by it, we can use FOR. Thus:

FOR. (*a*) *The train for Paris* (the train that is planned to go to Paris), *a ship bound for Rio, We're just starting (off* or *out) for the north, going for a holiday. Go for a walk, a swim, a drive, for pleasure, for what purpose? What for? We shall be out for dinner, we're having chicken for dinner.*

(*b*) *This is a present for you—I bought it to give to you. And this is for John. I'm doing this for you* (for your benefit, or on your behalf). *I'm asking (calling, looking, longing, sending) for you—* the object and purpose of those actions. *I'm sorry for you* (I'm giving you my sympathy). Notice the extension of this usage in *I'm FOR you* (giving you my support), *I'm for the motion* (giving my support to a proposal in a debate).

(*c*) With time, *for* + a measurement of time can indicate the proposed, expected or completed length of the period during which an action takes place: *We shall be staying in Scotland for three weeks. You've been learning English for six years. You were at school for twelve years. We walked for two hours. I shall love you for ever.*

309. *For* can also indicate exchange; e.g. *I bought this for ten dollars. May I change it for a slightly smaller one? You couldn't get anything smaller for love nor money. Thank you for your help.*

of

310. *From*, like *to*, basically expresses a physical movement, clearly traceable. The idea of *from* can be expressed in a more general, abstract way by OF, to indicate origin or one of the relationships defined in **311** below. Examine the following pairs:

(a) *This cupboard was made from (or out of) an old wooden packing-case. (A specific, clearly traceable transition.)*

It is therefore made of wood. (The transition from substance to object is less obvious, more general.)

(b) *These are all vegetables from (or out of) my garden.*

They are the fruits of the earth, results of my labours.

(c) *Fill the bucket from the well.*

The bucket's full of water.

(d) *Take some paper from my writing-pad.*

Have you taken a piece of my writing-pad?

(e) *Have a chocolate—take one from the bottom layer.*

I won't have another of yours— you have one of mine.

(f) *Your holiday didn't do you much good—you've lost all the colour from your cheeks already.*

Colour of eyes. Colour of hair (quoted from my passport).

(g) *I could make you a beautiful vase from this lump of clay.*

Are you making a fool of me, making fun of me?

311. An important function of *of* is to express the relationship between the part and the whole, e.g. *some of all, a quarter of an hour*. Variations of this are: the relationships between the member and the body to which that member belongs (*the leg of a chair, the top of the stairs, the secretary of the club*); between a quality and something possessing it (*the beauty of the landscape*); between a condition and something in that condition (*the health of a nation*); between an aspect and the thing we are considering (*a view of the summit*: cf. *a view from the summit*); and so on. *Of* is like the line in a fraction in mathematics. In $\frac{3}{8}, \frac{8}{3}, \frac{x}{y}, \frac{y}{x}$, the line tells us the relationship between 3 and 8, x and y, so long as we understand the significance of the order of the symbols, i.e. whether they come above or below the line. In *a brick of the house* (*Shakespeare lived in*) and *a house of brick*, the *of* indicates a similar relationship between *brick* and *house*, a relationship dependent on which word comes before *of* and which after it.

by, beyond, past, before, after

312. Look again at the diagram in **303**. Suppose we alter the position of the arrows and the small circle, so that the diagram looks like this:

145

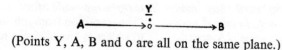

(Points Y, A, B and o are all on the same plane.)

FIG. 35

The movement now is in one direction only, although it may stop at o. Suppose X moves, in space, from A to B. In the process, *X goes B Y the point Y*. At o, X is stationary: *it is then B Y the point Y*. Notice that it goes not only as far as Y (**305**), but also BEYOND it. To emphasise that, in going by Y, X goes beyond it, we can say that *X goes PAST Y*.

313.   In time, the first arrow in **312** begins at A, which is BEFORE Y, and *ends B Y Y*. In this sense, *by* can be analysed to mean *in the progress of time ending about but not later than* the point of time mentioned. Compare *by* with *till* in the following pair of sentences:

   (*a*) *I shall not be ready till five o'clock*—my not being ready will extend through a period ending at that point, when I *shall* be ready.
   (*c*) *I shall not be ready by five o'clock*—i.e. I shall not be ready in a period ending at five.

314. In the diagram in **312**, B is AFTER Y; in other words, at B, time has gone past Y, and in that sense *B is past Y*; thus *it is half past eleven, past my bedtime*. Continuous progress of time, past Y, then past a new point, Z, etc., can be said to go on *by day* and *by night*.

315.   It may be stretching the imagination too far to fit *by* as an expression of *means* or *agency* into this scheme. If only for convenience and to complete the picture, I would classify this aspect of *by* as a spatial relationship represented by the second part of the movement in **312.** It is easy enough to see that the train, in **303,** goes from London to Edinburgh BY York. The next step, if the reader can take it, is to see that the traveller goes from London to Edinburgh *by York*, and *by train*. To go back to the diagram in **312**, Y is the means *by* which X proceeds from A *to B*, the means by which B is attained. (Compare this with *with*, **335**.) This stretch of the imagination could enable us to account for usages on the pattern of *by means of*, *by electricity*, and also *a book by Conan Doyle*, i.e. the medium by which the book was created; but it could not easily account for other usages, such as *This room measures 6 metres by 4.*

146

316. Examples of *by*:

BY. (*a*) in space, continuous movement passing Y: *I always go by the post-office on my way to the station.*

(*b*) in space, fixed relationship with and very near Y: *He was sitting by the fire, by the open window, by his mother, by himself* (i.e. alone). For *walking along by the river*, see **319.**

(*c*) in space—means or agency: *We'll manage this somehow— by hook or by crook. To travel by car, by air, by sea. To send a message by ordinary mail, by telephone, by radio. To learn something by heart, by chance. Material made by hand, by machinery. 'Ode to a Nightingale', by John Keats.*

(*d*) in time, ending near, and not past, Y: '*Cobbler, cobbler, mend my shoe, Get it done by half past two.*' (Nursery rhyme.) *The concert will be over by ten.*

(*e*) in time, passing one stage after another: *To avoid being seen, they travelled by night, and lay hidden during the day.*

round, about

317. X can go ROUND Y,

(*a*)

like *a fence round a tree*; or

(*b*)

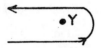

like *a yacht sailing round a buoy*; or

(*c*)

FIG. 36

like *a man walking round the corner.*

147

Around has the same meaning as *round*, and can be substituted for it for the sake of rhythm, e.g. to avoid two stressed syllables coming together. In space, ABOUT, as a concrete expression of **317** (*a*), is now out of fashion. Shakespeare's Julius Caesar said: 'Let me have men about me that are fat.' In modern English, this would be 'I must have men around me', or 'round about me' if one wanted to reinforce the idea of having such men on every side. However, as an adverbial particle, *about* is still used in the sense of (*a*) and even of (*b*)—as in **343.** In the abstract, *about* commonly suggests '*moving in any direction, or being in any position, in the vicinity of the point*'; e.g. *think, talk, know, dream about the subject; tell me all about it; don't worry about it; what is it about? A book, or a lecture, about mountaineering* suggests a general treatment of the subject and freedom to wander a little from the point; whereas *a book, or a lecture, on new techniques in rock-climbing*, suggests concentration on a clearly defined field. In time, *I'll be there about six o'clock* is a common usage, expressing the idea of (*a*). We can also say *I'll be there around six o'clock.*

One dimension

to, on, from, off

318.   Now apply the scheme to a line:

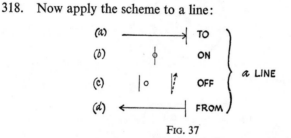

FIG. 37

Examples:

(*a*) *This road leads to the river, to the coast, to the frontier.*

(*b*) *London is on the River Thames. Brighton is on the coast. I'm on my way home. Am I on the right road for Y? Never stand on the edge of a cliff.* (Note, however: *Will there be a customs examination at the frontier?* i.e. at the point on the frontier where our road crosses it.)

(*c*) *You're not on the right road for X—but you're not far off it. The 'Titanic' was wrecked off the coast of Greenland. A man was killed last night when his car skidded off the road and crashed into a tree.*

(*d*) *Refugees fleeing from the frontier. Stand away from the edge.*

along

319.   When we say *X is on the road to* Y, we are more concerned with X's position than with its movement. To emphasise the idea of movement following the course before it, we say *X is moving ALONG the road to* Y. Thus:

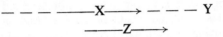

X is moving along the path to Y. Notice Z (on the same plane) which is moving along by, or beside, it.

across

320.   Apply the diagram in **312** to a line, either thus:

(*a*)   — BY, BESIDE

or thus:

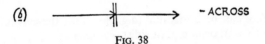

(*b*)   — ACROSS

FIG. 38

(*a*) could represent *a man walking* BY (*or* BESIDE) *a river,* or *walking along by,* or *along beside, it;* or, at o, *a man standing by,* or *beside, the river.*

(*b*) could represent *a road running ACROSS the frontier,* or *a tree lying across the railway-line.*

behind, in front of

321.   In the following situation

X — A — B → Y

A is BEHIND B, and B is IN FRONT OF A. This applies both when the arrow represents the line of vision of a speaker at X, and when it represents a line of advance along which A and B are moving in the direction indicated.

Two dimensions, producing area

on (or on to), on, off

322.   Movement in the direction of a surface, and reaching it, is expressed by ON. To emphasise movement towards, and then position on, the surface, or the effort required to complete this process, we say ON TO. (This is sometimes written *onto*, by a reasonable analogy with *into*, but *onto* is not accepted by conservative grammarians: students would be safer writing *on to*.) To indicate that X (moving or stationary) covers some or all of the surface Y, we use ON. The opposite of *on to*, and the negative of *on* (i.e. *not on*) is OFF.

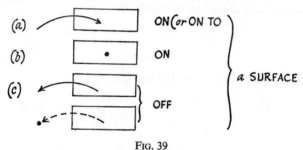

Fig. 39

The surface can be horizontal (e.g. the floor, the ceiling); it can be vertical (a wall); or lateral (a side). Examples:

(*a*) *Have you put the bread on the table?* (movement, but *on to* unnecessary). *This suitcase is terribly heavy. Can you help me lift it on to the bed?* (*on to* emphasising movement in that direction, then placing on the surface); *Hang the pictures on the wall.*

(*b*) *Is the bread on the table? How can I sleep with this suitcase on the bed? Don't run on the flower-beds. Keep on the right side of the law.*

(*c*) *Help me get this suitcase off the bed again. Keep your feet off the chairs.*

323.   As we noticed with *talk about v talk on* (**317**), *on* concentrates on a more clearly defined field: a field is a surface having length and breadth. Moreover, while *X is at Y* suggests that X occupies more or less the same position as Y, without specifying dimension, *X is on Y* indicates that X covers some if not all of the actual surface of Y, or is supported by it, or is attached to it. Example: *There was no policeman at the spot where the accident occurred, but the police were on the spot within two minutes,* i.e. they were standing on the actual scene of the accident. *To be at business* means to be at work in an office;

150

to go to New York on business is to go there with a specified field of business to cover. One can be *at the point of leaving*; or *on the point of leaving*, like a runner on his marks. (The starter of a race calls out: '*On your marks—get set . . .*' and fires the starting-pistol.) *A fish, nibbling at your bait, is not yet on your hook.* From all this, it should be easy to understand *a hat on one's head, a house on the top of the hill, riding on horseback, standing on one's own feet*—and hence *to travel on foot.*

324. With time, note: *at six o'clock O N a sunny day in June, on* covering a division of time intermediate between that associated with *at* and that with *in*. Similarly, *on Monday, on Tuesday*, etc., *on the morning (afternoon, evening) of the third day.* Observe the difference between *Where were you on the morning of November 19th?* i.e. on that precise date, and *On November 19th, I was working at my office in the morning, but went home feeling unwell in the afternoon* (see *in*, **329**).

325. O N can therefore be used:

   (*a*) with reference to a line, **318** (*b*);

   (*b*) to show X moving towards, and reaching, a surface, horizontal or vertical, **322** (*a*);

   (*c*) to show X at rest, partially or wholly covering Y, or supported by it, **322** (*b*) and **323**; and

   (*d*) with reference to time, in establishing the date of an event, precise to the day of the week or month.

326. *Upon* is sometimes substituted for *on to* (movement) and *on* (rest) in dignified or poetic language, for the sake of rhythm, or to suggest 'firmly on' or 'high up on'; cf., however, *up on*, **347**. *Upon* occurs in certain fixed expressions, like the exclamatory *upon my word, upon my soul*, though these may now be going out of fashion.

327. Other relationships with an object having area are:

(*a*)

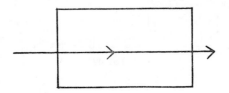

FIG. 40

A road running A C R O S S the plain (cf. **320**, *b*)

151

(b)

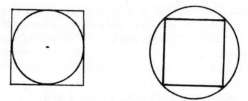

FIG. 41

*The first circle goes RO UN D the inside of the square,
the second round the outside of it.*

Three dimensions, having volume

**in (or into), in (or inside),
out of, outside**

328. In space, movement in the direction of a space and penetrating it is expressed, simply, by IN; but to mark the emphasis comparable to that expressed by *on to* we say INTO a space. To indicate that X occupies some or all of the space Y, we use IN. The opposite of *into* is OUT OF. The negative of the preposition *in* (i.e. *not in*) is OUTSIDE. To emphasise the idea of *not outside* we use INSIDE.

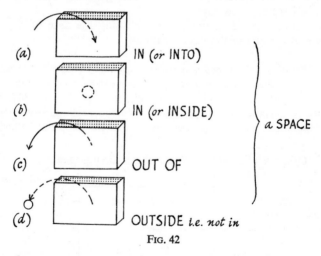

FIG. 42

Examples:

(a) *Put these books in your suitcase* (movement, but *into* unnecessary). *People started running into the building* (*into* emphasising the complete movement, and also necessary to avoid confusion with *running in the building* which might suggest running inside, not outside it.

(*b*) *Is my book in your suitcase? Shakespeare was born in England, in Warwickshire. I don't like swimming in muddy water, nor in the dark. Wait inside the car till the rain stops.*

(*c*) *They all rushed out of the building again when the explosion occurred.*

(*d*) *Outside the house, the crowd watched anxiously.*

in, within

329. Whereas *X is on* Y suggests that Y *supports* X, *X is IN* Y suggests that Y *encloses* X: in other words, Y has limits which hold X. Imagine and demonstrate the difference between *I place this coin on my hand* and *What have I got in my hand?* Such limits may enclose a surface-area; but in saying *in this area* (*district, region*), *in this city, in Africa*, etc., the emphasis is not on the supporting surface but on the space enclosed by certain limits. Emphasis on the idea of *in* certain limits and not outside them is contained in the word WITHIN which can be used for space (*within an area*) or time (*within six days*).

330. There are many metaphorical applications of the above uses of *in*. Examples: *To be in debt, in love, in trouble, in good health. This book is written in English.*

in, during

331. In time, *in* is used with a period, thus: *Classes start in October. He was born in 1846, in the nineteenth century.* Note *Rome was not built in a day*, i.e. it was not built within the limits of twenty-four hours. (However, optimism, or incapacity to fulfil a promise, often leads us to say *I'll be with you in a moment*, or *in three days' time* when the chances are that the event will take place just within the final limits of the period, or even later.) *He ran a mile in 4 minutes* means that his running took exactly that time. DURING is used to indicate the continuance or the extent of an event or series of events, in relation to the period named; e.g. *The entrance examinations will be held during September.* The difference between *in* and *during* might be shown thus:

153

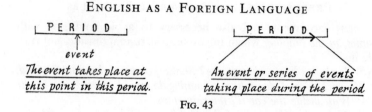

The event takes place at this point in this period.

An event or series of events taking place during the period

FIG. 43

332. Comparable with *passing by a point*, or *across a line or surface*, we have *THROUGH a space or period*, thus:

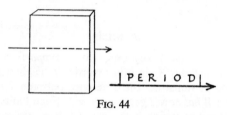

FIG. 44

Knock a hole through the wall.   *All through the night.*

Different levels

up, down; over, under, underneath; above, below, beneath

333. UP (↑) and DOWN (↓) should raise no difficulty; nor should

OVER   and

UNDER

Compare *a roof over one's head*, i.e. providing cover or protection, with *a hat on one's head*, i.e. touching, and supported by, its surface; similarly, compare *a fly on the ceiling*, i.e. attached to it and *a dog under the table*, i.e. covered by it. The idea of being physically covered up can be emphasised by *UNDERNEATH*, e.g. *I found this important letter underneath a pile of newspapers.* ABOVE stresses the idea of *at a higher point* or *on a higher level*; BELOW, *a lower point or level.* A swimmer has to keep his head *above water*: what is important is that his mouth should be at a higher level than the water's surface. A skin-diver must be careful not to go *below* a certain depth otherwise the pressure at that lower level will cause him serious injury. A man can be *above me* or *below me* in rank, without being *over me* or *under me*, i.e. without directly controlling me or having to obey my orders. Emphasis on the idea of the lowness of the level is contained in BENEATH, especially in poetic and metaphorical expressions, as in *beneath the waves, beneath contempt.*

154

334. *Over* and *under* express both rest and motion. *Over* often expresses the following movement:

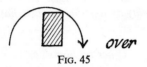

FIG. 45

and often emphasises the idea of having arrived at the other side of an obstacle; e.g. 'The cow jumped over the moon' (nursery rhyme) and *You're over the line*, i.e. you've crossed it.

Relationships between forces

with, without, against

335. Now consider relationships between the forces represented by the arrows in **301**, thus:

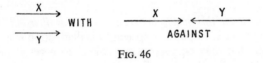

FIG. 46

In Fig. 46, *X is going WITH Y*. The negative of this statement is, of course, *X is not going with Y*: in other words, *it is going WITH-OUT Y*. Physically, the opposite of it (Fig. 46), is *X is going AGAINST Y*. Note the difference between *Come and sit by me*, i.e. occupy the position illustrated by o in **312**, and *Come and sit with me (and we shall proceed together)*. Note also the instrumental *with*, and compare it with the *by* of means or agency. When you *write with a pen*, your hand and pen proceed together.

336. On the other hand, when you *swim against the current*, you and the current are in conflict. Even when you are *leaning against the wall*, there is a force against you: if that force is not strong enough, the wall collapses. *One fights against temptation, struggles against fierce opposition, produces arguments against one's opponents in a debate*. Nevertheless—partly, perhaps, for reasons connected with the derivation of the word *with*—one can still *fight with an adversary, struggle with a problem, argue with one's wife*: in such cases, one might imagine oneself and one's adversary proceeding together in the same movement, the same furious dance. But notice how this apparent confusion is clarified in the following example:

155

in a game of bridge, North and South are playing with East and West. To make it clear who are partners and who are opponents, we say *North is playing with South, East is playing with West,* and *North and South are playing together against East and West.*

Other relationships

between, among

337. X may stand or move BETWEEN two objects, Y and Z, thus:

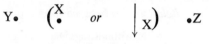

FIG. 47

or AMONG *more than two.*

Note *I can divide this money between you two* or *distribute it among* (or *amongst*) *you all.* In popular speech, this distinction is not always clearly made and may be becoming weaker: as a result *between* is often used for *more than two.* Even speakers consciously applying a rule and endeavouring to restrict *between* to two things only, would feel it unnatural to do so when discussing, for example, *the difference between various factors,* although in such a situation they might be thinking of the difference between only two factors at a time, i.e. between X and Y, and then between X (or Y) and Z.

like, as

338. In comparing one thing with another, we may find that *X is LIKE Y,* or *UNLIKE* it. A distinction is made, and still insisted upon by grammarians, between the preposition *like,* which indicates a relationship between objects, and the conjunction *as* joining two statements; e.g. *John walks just like his father,* but *He walks just as his father used to* (*walk*). Most grammarians would consider it 'incorrect' to use *like* in the second example, although it is becoming a common 'mistake' among native-speakers of English. Traditional grammar would not classify *as* as a preposition—even in the phrase you have just read. Yet it is difficult not to consider *as* with the other little words in this chapter. Take the example: *As a speaker, he was brilliant.* It does not help us very much to be told that *as a speaker*

156

really means *when he acts as a speaker acts*: in modern English, *as* in such an example is merely a convenient way of saying *in the role of*, or something similar. However grammarians may classify *as*, the student will no doubt want to see the difference between, say, *He spoke to me like a father* (comparison) and *He wrote to me as my legal adviser* (in that role or capacity).

Freedom of choice

339.   One can arrive at a point on the map (*We arrived at the station five minutes earlier*), arrive on what one sees as a surface (*We arrived on the platform just as the train was coming in*), or arrive in a space (*We arrived in London late last night*). One can be *on a chair* or *in a chair*, according to whether the speaker has in mind the surface of the seat or the space contained by the seat, the back and the arms. One can be *in bed* on a cold night, or can rest *on the bed* on a hot afternoon (for *in bed v on the bed*, see **115**). One can drive *across London*, or *through it*, according to whether one sees it as a surface-area or a conglomeration of streets and buildings.

Influence of Latin and Greek

340.   The Latin prepositions—*ab* (= from), *ad* (= to), *cum* (= with), *de* (= from), *ex, e* (= from, out of), and the Greek *sym* (= with), absorbed into English words as prefixes, tend to attract the English prepositions which are supposed to be equivalent in meaning to the words from which the prefixes were derived. Thus: *absent from, adhere to, communicate with, different from, exempt from, sympathise with*. With *different* there would appear to be a conflict between etymology, which requires the preposition *from*, and the tendencies in modern English which I am trying to trace in this chapter. Many native-English speakers, uninhibited by a strict grammatical teaching, point from one thing to another, and remark that *this is different to that*. That is natural and logical, even if it is incorrect by traditional rules. On the other hand, *depend on* (cf. *hang on*) is recognised as 'correct', although speakers of languages derived from Latin are being consistent etymologically when they say *'depend from'. With words of this kind, be careful to observe what the direct object of the prefix is: for example, in *The dishonest cashier absconded with the cash*, *absconded* means 'go or hide away *from* somewhere', and in that example *with* is a straightforward usage as in **335**. Note, similarly, *appeal (to someone) for a donation*.

157

Mechanical Associations

341.   While the foregoing paragraphs in this chapter may provide some form of systematisation for the English prepositions, a great many usages can only be mastered by mechanical association, especially where the idea of movement or position in space is very weak or absent altogether. The student must simply observe such associations as *afraid of* (*nothing*), *believe in* (*miracles*), *suffer from* (*an illness*), *congratulate* (*you*) *on* (*your success*), *grateful for* (*small mercies*), and get into the habit of forming them himself automatically. He must not be surprised, however, if he finds that in some of these purely mechanical associations even native-English usage can be uncertain and conflicting.

Prepositions in relative clauses, and questions

342.   All the prepositions can fit into the following patterns:

(*a*) *I am referring to the question of your debts.*
(*b*) *That is the question to which I am referring.*
(*c*) *That's the question I'm re'ferring to.*

(*b*) is more formal; and, in spoken English, sounds clumsy and unnatural; (*c*), more colloquial, though becoming increasingly acceptable in writing. In the interrogative, note

(*d*) *To what are you re'ferring?* (note as for *b*).
(*e*) *What are you re'ferring to?* (note as for *c*).

Adverbial Particles

343.   Do not confuse the preposition separated from its object, as in **342,** with the adverbial particle, which indicates a movement or position in space or time without direct reference to an object. Most of the prepositions can be used as adverbial particles, but not all of them can be. Study this table:

Preposition	Adverbial Particle
Walk across the street.	*How can we get A'CROSS?*
I saw him coming along the road.	*Come A'LONG.*
Who is that behind you?	*Don't be left BE'HIND.*
My cabin is below the main deck.	*I'm going BE'LOW.*
I passed by your window.	*Why pass 'BY?*
Similarly, down the hill.	*Go 'DOWN.*
in front of me.	*Keep IN 'FRONT.*

in the car.	*Get 'IN*
inside the house.	*Stay IN'SIDE.*
Get off the bus.	*Get 'OFF 'quickly.*
Get on the bus.	*Get 'ON again.*
Go out of the room.	*Go 'OUT.*
Outside the house.	*Go 'OUT'SIDE.*
Jump over the gate.	*Jump 'OVER.*
Drive past the school.	*Drive 'PAST*
Since New Year.	*I haven't seen him 'SINCE.*
through the hole.	*How can I get 'THROUGH?*
under the rope.	*Can you crawl 'UNDER (or UNDER-'NEATH)?*
up the hill again.	*But don't run 'UP.*

Notice *run ABOUT*, i.e. 'run in various directions'; *ABOUT turn*, in marching, i.e. 'turn and go the opposite way'; and *turn ROUND*, i.e. perform one of the movements illustrated in **317**. *Turn OVER* expresses the movement illustrated in **334**. This movement could make a complete circle and continue thus, as in *a log rolling over and over* or *saying the same thing over and over again*. In *the war is over* (i.e. ended) or in *I've finished my shopping and have two pounds over* (i.e. remaining), we are concerned with the termination of the movement in **334**. Note the special uses of *off* and *out*, in *set off* (i.e. off the starting-line, start on a journey) and *set out* (i.e. out of one's home or one's base, also at the beginning of a journey); *look out* (from one's base) and *point out*; also of *down*, in *turn down*, *break down*.

344. The adverbial particles thus express movement or positions in space and time similar to those expressed by the corresponding prepositions. The following are seldom, if ever, used as adverbial particles: *to, at, from, towards, till, for, of, into, during, with, without, against*, though the nouns that follow can sometimes be omitted and understood, as in *Are you for the motion* (i.e. proposal in a debate), *or against?* Note also *come 'to* (recover from unconsciousness) and *go* or *do without* (something). On the other hand, there are two important particles with no corresponding prepositions, namely AWAY and BACK, e.g. *Don't go AWAY. Please come BACK.*

Adverbial Particles as 'Gestures'

345. Native-English speakers are restrained in the use of gestures with their hands but something like the equivalent of gesture might be noticeable in the use of little words like *on, in, up, off*, and *out*.

159

One might imagine in such words reflection of *vocal* gesture: thus, the combination of sounds in *on*, with its liquid consonant, could represent *continuity*; the weak vowel in *in*, plus the liquid, could suggest *collapse*; the short vowel plus plosive in *up* could be a stimulus of arousal; or the stop-sound in *up* could indicate cessation. Thus:

ON—continuity, movement forward ⟶

> e.g. *go on, keep on, lead on, carry on, play on.* A light or tap can be *on* (opposite, *off*).

IN—collapse ↘

> e.g. *give in;* colloquial *done in* or *all in* (exhausted).

UP—arousal ↗

> *speak up, play up, keep up* (i.e. don't fall behind), *poke the fire up* (to make it burn more brightly).

UP—stoppage ↗|

> *give up, hold up* (i.e. delay), *the game's up* (it's no good struggling any longer).

Then notice the connection between sound and sense in OFF, as in *The firework went off almost in my face.* OUT could be linked with a gesture suggesting a sudden or a wide opening, as in *burst out* (*laughing*), *spread out* (*far and wide*); or, with its diminishing diphthong ending in a hardly audible *t*, it could suggest disappearance, as in *blow out* (*the light*), *burn out, die out.*

Up, out—completion of the act

346. See Chapter Eight, **216.**

Adverbial Particle + Preposition

347. It frequently happens, especially in spoken English, that direction and position are indicated by an adverbial particle (or even two particles) followed immediately by a preposition. Examples:

I'm just going across to the grocer's (i.e. across the road to . . .); or *over to the grocer's* (i.e. over the road).

I'll come along to the station with you (along the road).
Go down to the kitchen (downstairs).
John's gone off to school quite happily.
He's gone up to the senior school now.
Can you help me get up on to the roof?
We must have something in reserve to fall back on.

Verb + Preposition or Particle

348.   What are sometimes called 'phrasal verbs', i.e. constructions consisting of verbs plus the little words we have been discussing in this chapter, are very frequently used in English, especially in the spoken language, and give the student a good deal of trouble. In the main, these constructions consist of the verb *to be* or a simple verb expressing physical action—e.g. *go, come, put, take, give, get, do, make, let, keep, send, bring, stand, fall, sit, turn, break, tear, throw, walk, run, jump*—followed by a little word expressing direction or position.

349.   The student should have no difficulty in understanding *Mr. Smith is in, out, away, back. He has gone (or come) in, out, inside, outside, up, down. It's raining—put the chairs inside. It's stopped—take them out again. I've given away all my money. How can I get it back again? You'll have to do without. Please let me in— don't keep me out in the rain. Don't stop—keep on. I'll keep in front— you keep up with the rest of the party. Send my breakfast up to my room. Bring it back, I haven't finished. I'll send it round to your office. Stand up, stand outside. Don't fall down, don't fall over. Sit down, but sit up straight. Turn round, turn over. Thieves broke in. Fire broke out. Who's torn up my paper? Who's torn down the notice I put up on the board? Walk out quietly. 'The dish ran away with the spoon.' A dog running along behind the car.*

350.   These phrases tend to become fixed expressions with special meanings. Thus, in the morning I *wake up, get up* and am then *up* (i.e. out of bed). My bedroom is on the second floor: I am upstairs. I go downstairs, and am then *down*. I *put on* my hat and go out. The streets are crowded: I try to *get on* (i.e. make progress) but am *held up* (delayed) by the traffic. So I *make up* my mind to go back till the rush is over. That is simple enough, and the student can easily get into the habit of using such expressions. The meaning may not be so obvious, though it should now be understandable, in phrases like *Stand up to him, don't be afraid, fight back. I'll try, but I don't feel*

up to it (i.e. capable of it). *I'll stand up for you* (defend you), *I won't let you down* (I won't fail to support you). *I've given you my word and I won't go back on it. We'll see this through together* (will go through this experience, and finish it, together: cf. *Mr. Britling Sees it Through*, by H. G. Wells). *We won't give up the struggle: if there are difficulties, we'll put up with them* (i.e. give up worrying about them, and stop or stay *with* them). To *put up* at a hotel for the night is to stop on one's journey and stay there.

'Separated' and 'Non-separated' Patterns*

351.   Care should be taken to distinguish between particles expressing, directly or remotely, direction or position, and prepositions expressing relationships in space or time between one thing and another thing. That 'other thing' is traditionally said to be 'governed' by the preposition. Notice the difference between

(*a*) *Take off your hat.*
and
(*b*) *Take that hat off your head.*

In (*a*), *off* does not 'govern' hat: it only indicates the direction in which the hat must be moved. In (*b*), *off* 'governs' head, in so far as it indicates a relationship between *hat* and *head*. In (*a*) *off* can come before or after the direct object, *hat*. In (*b*), *off* can only come before the noun it governs. This explains the so-called 'separated' and 'non-separated' patterns, examples of which are given below.

'Separated'

(i)   *Call 'in the doctor, call the doctor 'in, call him 'in.*
(ii) *Call 'up the reserves, call the reserves 'up, call them 'up.*
(iii) *Look 'up this word in the dictionary, look this word 'up in the dictionary, look it 'up in the dictionary.*

In these examples, *in* and *up* are particles, not prepositions governing *doctor, reserves, word.*

'Non-separated'

(iv) *'Call at the 'hospital and see how the patient is.*
(v) *'Crawl up the 'slope.*
(vi) *'Look up the 'chimney.*

* These terms are used in *English Sentence Patterns* by Robert Lado and Charles C. Fries, Ann Arbor, The University of Michigan Press.

Here, *at* and *up* are prepositions, governing *hospital, slope, chimney,* i.e. indicate a relationship between the person addressed and the objects named. Remember (**219**) that the 'separated pattern' is only 'separated' in so far as the particle can come before or after the direct object (unless the direct object is a pronoun, in which case the particle must come after). If there is no direct object, separation does not occur; e.g. *We set off at dawn, We started out too early.*

CHAPTER TWELVE

Notes On Word Order

352. Word order, and the patterns commonly used in English utterances and written sentences, are a very important aspect of the language, though they do not come within the scope of this book, except incidentally. Students using this book should observe the sentence patterns followed in the examples (as well as in the text), just as in listening to the spoken tongue they should assimilate the patterns of stress and intonation.

353. Study the word order in the sentences below:
   (*a*) *The old man opened the door slowly.*
   (*b*) *He was very old.*
   (*c*) *He was often there late at night.*
   (*d*) *He always went to the door every morning.*
   (*e*) *No one paid him any attention.*
   (*f*) *No one paid any attention to the poor old man.*

If we assume these to be normal English sentence-patterns, we can draw certain conclusions from them, e.g. the Subject (*the old man*) precedes the Predicate (*opened the door slowly*); the adjective accompanying the noun in the subject precedes the noun; the direct object (*the door*) immediately follows the verb (*opened*); the adverb comes at the end. The reader is invited to draw similar conclusions regarding the adjective as a complement of the verb *to be* in example (*b*); the relative positions of the adverbs of frequency (*often, always*), the adverbials of place (*there, to the door*) and the adverbials of time (*late at night, every morning*) in (*c*) and (*d*); the relative position of the direct object (*any attention*) and the indirect object without a preposition (*him*), or with a preposition (*to the poor old man*) in (*e*) and (*f*). The reader is then left puzzling out the relative position of *poor* and *old*.

354. The patterns in **353** can be deliberately altered for the sake of

emphasis or contrast, or for the sake of balance, or to avoid ambiguity. E.g:

(*a*) *We must examine carefully the meanings of the words we use* (from a broadcast by Rex Warner).

(*b*) *A hundred years ago, women were, in the eyes of the law, chattels* (from a broadcast talk by Violet Markham).

The student should remember that these variations to the 'normal' order are made purposely; and if there is no purpose in them they are out of place.

355. A special problem is that of the position of adverbs. Note:

(*a*) *SLOWLY, the old man opened the door.*

(*b*) *He opened the door.*

(*c*) *He SLOWLY opened the door.*

(*d*) *He opened the door SLOWLY.*

All these arrangements are acceptable.* Now notice what questions could produce these arrangements as answers:

(*a*) *Slowly, what did the old man do?*

(*b*) *What did he do?*

(*c*) *What exactly did he do?*

(*d*) *How did he open the door?*

(The substitution of *it* for *the door* would not affect the position of the adverb.)

356. From **355**, we may conclude that the adverb can come at the beginning, in the middle, or at the end of the sentence. If it comes at the beginning, it is specially picked out from the sentence, to give us some information in advance, to set the scene for the action that follows. If it comes in the middle, it only qualifies, and does not substantially add to, the information produced by such a question as *What did he do?*—though it may tell us he never did it at all. In other words, the adverb in the medial position illustrates some *aspect* of the verb. But if the adverb comes at the end of the sentence, it provides more than a modification of the verb and answers a new question. The end-position adverb adds to the information already given us in the sentence by telling us *how, how often, when* or *where* the event occurred. Moreover, when the adverb occupies the mid-position emphasis tends to fall on the verb (e.g. *This is what I nor-*

---

* What would not be acceptable would be to place *slowly* between *opened* and *the door* (or *it*); but note, in accordance with **354**, *He opened, very slowly, the most amazing book I have ever seen.*

mally say); when it occupies the end-position, emphasis is more on the adverb (*This is what I say normally*).*

357. The mid-position adverb is thus intimately connected with the verb, and is almost part of it. It is as though the verb were, say, *to slowly-shut*. Fear of the grammarian's taboo on the 'split' infinitive, as it is called, deterred me from omitting the hyphen between *slowly* and *shut*. Nevertheless, *I want you to creep downstairs and then to quietly shut the door* is perfectly natural spoken English, *quietly shut* being a refinement of *shut*, just as *creep* is a refinement of *go*. This is relevant to so-called *adverbs of frequency*, e.g. *always, often, sometimes, seldom*, which are associated with verbal aspects (see Chapter Seven), in so far as they draw attention to a series of acts (*I always go, often go*) or to an unending process (*You are always tapping on the table*). It is also relevant to *adverbs of degree*, e.g. *almost, hardly, nearly, quite, just,†* which indicate the degree to which an act is completed (again see Chapter Seven); e.g. *I nearly forgot to tell you*. In short *I want you to always remember* and *You'll have to almost break it to get it open*, though they would incur some grammarians' and many examiners' displeasure,‡ are not only natural English but are good examples of *always* and *almost* as indicators of verbal aspect.

358. Some adverbs of frequency and of degree can serve either the mid-position function or the end function. E.g:

(a) *Do you go to the theatre? Yes, I do. I often do.*
(b) *How many times a year do you go to the theatre? Oh, I don't know how many times, but I go quite often.*

* Change of position could also produce a quite different meaning; e.g. *He generally* (i.e. usually) *does much better than that*, but *I'm speaking generally* (i.e. in general terms). Note also *Quite properly*, i.e. as was right and proper,`He was punished*, but *He was punished properly* (in the right way, with no half-measures).

† *Almost* suggests approach, nearing accomplishment (———→); *hardly* a negative nearness—not there yet; *nearly*, a short distance away from accomplishment, without the idea of approach. Non-nearness is expressed by *not nearly. Quite* suggests accomplishment achieved, or position or condition reached, e.g. *I quite understand*, though sometimes it can suggest 'to be on the point of accomplishment, etc.', e.g. *I quite like it but it isn't exactly what I want. Just* can be either an adverb of relative time, suggesting recent past, or an adverb of degree suggesting 'that act accomplished, or that point reached, no more and no less'. Thus *Your book? I've just seen it* could mean either that I've seen it recently, or only seen it, not read it. *He just ran away* could mean either that he ran away a moment ago, or that he ran and did not stop or walk.

‡ 'Correct' grammar would insist on *always to remember, almost to break*.

Note that whereas question (*a*) asks for a statement of activity, plain or qualified, question (*b*) requires a definite or emphatic statement of frequency. These classes of adverb can also be picked out and placed at the beginning of the sentence, if special emphasis or contrast has to be made and if it is clear to which verb the adverb will refer: e.g. *I never go without breakfast, but sometimes I only have a piece of toast.* However, if *never*, *seldom* or *rarely* opens the sentence, then inversion of verb and subject occur: *Never (seldom, rarely) have I seen such a sight.*

359. The table below may serve as a rough guide to the position of common types of adverb. Bold type indicates normal position. Ordinary type suggests alternative position for the sake of emphasis; or, at the beginning of the sentence, for the sake of contrast; or for the reason given in **357**. A gap warns the student that it would be unsafe for him to use the adverb concerned in that position. Note that when adverbials of place and time occur in the same sentence, the former precedes the latter so long as emphasis and comparative length of construction do not require it otherwise.

Position in the Sentence

Adverbs of—	Beginning	Middle	End
Manner	e.g. Quietly,	quietly	**quietly.**
Place	There,		**there.**
Time	Today,		**today.**
Relative Time	Already,	**already**	already.
		just	
	Soon,	**soon**	soon.
	(See*)	**still**	still.
		yet	**yet.**
	(Scarcely, with inversion)	**scarcely**	
Relative Frequency		**always**	always.
	Frequently,	**frequently**	frequently.
	Generally,	**generally**	(see †)
	Often,	**often**	often.
	Sometimes,	**sometimes**	sometimes.
	Usually,	**usually**	

* *Still*, at the beginning of a sentence usually serves in modern speech as a signal that the speaker is about to qualify a preceding statement; it might be replaced by *all the same*.
† *Generally* in this position usually means *in a general way*.

	Seldom	⎫	**seldom**	seldom.
	Rarely	⎬ with inversion	**rarely**	rarely.
	Hardly ever		**hardly ever**	
	Never	⎭	**never**	
Degree	Gradually,		**gradually**	*gradually*
			completely	**completely.**
			almost	
			hardly	
			scarcely	
			nearly (not nearly)	
			quite	
			just	
			even, never even	

Adverbs in Mid-Position

360. The adverb in mid-position comes immediately before a simple verb: *I often see him. It never even occurred to me.* Notice what happens with the verb *to be*, with compound tense-forms, auxiliaries and modal verbs:

(a) *He is usually late. He has seldom arrived on time.* But notice emphatic assertion in: *He isn't often late, is he? As a matter of fact, he usually* **is** *late.* Similarly, *He never* **has** *been early.*

(b) *I can well believe it* (= I can quite believe it. But *You can speak English* (*very*) *well.*)

(c) *You must never give up. We are gradually getting there.*

(d) *I have hardly ever seen him, have never even spoken to him.*

(e) *We have nearly* (*almost*) (*quite*) *finished.*

(f) *We've not nearly* (*we've hardly or scarcely*) (*we've not quite*) *finished.*

(g) *You would never guess what happened.*

(h) *I could hardly have imagined it possible.*

Look for it, look it up

361. For the position of the preposition and adverbial particle in constructions like *look for, look . . . up*, see **219** and **351**. The relative position of prepositions, adverbial particles, object and adverb are shown in the following examples:

Notes on Word Order

(*a*) *Phrase containing a preposition which must govern an object.*

> *Look for the answer. Look for it.*
> *Look very carefully for the answer,* or
> *Look for the answer very carefully.*

(*b*) *Phrase containing an adverbial particle expressing direction or 'gesture', not governing the object.*

> *Look up the word in your dictionary,* or
> *Look the word up in your dictionary.*
> *Look it up in your dictionary* (no alternative order).

INDEX OF GRAMMATICAL POINTS TREATED

Principal subjects are printed in capitals; others in ordinary type; words used as examples in italics. Abbreviations, etc.:

adj. = adjective; ff. = and following sections; fn. = footnote; inf. = infinitive; -ing = participle or gerund; N. = note; part. = adverbial particle; passim = everywhere; prep. = preposition; ref. = reference; — = head-word repeated, e.g. (*decide to*), — *on -ing* = *decide on* (*do*)*ing*. Numbers refer to sections, not pages; those in bold type to principal sections.

170

172

GEORGE ALLEN & UNWIN LTD

London: 40 Museum Street, W.C.1

Auckland: 24 Wyndham Street
Bombay: 15 Graham Road, Ballard Estate, Bombay 1
Buenos Aires: Escritorio 454-459, Florida 165
Calcutta: 17 Chittaranjan Avenue, Calcutta 13
Cape Town: 109 Long Street
Hong Kong: Fl/12 Mirador Mansions, Kowloon
Ibadan: P.O. Box 62
Karachi: Karachi Chambers, McLeod Road
Madras: Mohan Mansion, 38c Mount Road, Madras 6
Mexico: Villalongin 32-10, Piso, Mexico 5, D.F.
Nairobi: P.O. Box 12446
New Delhi: 13-14 Ajmeri Gate Extension, New Delhi 1
São Paulo: Avenida 9 De Julho 1138-Ap. 51
Singapore: 36c Prinsep Street, Singapore 7
Sydney, N.S.W.: Bradbury House, 55 York Street
Toronto: 91 Wellington Street West

MARIO PEI

THE STORY OF LANGUAGE

Here is a book, quite free of the odour of the schoolroom, which tells the story of language, as fully as it can be told in the compass of 500 pages, and tells it with humour and commonsense.

The Story of Language is a volume which can be read aloud to the family; it can be studied carefully; it can be kept on the shelf next to the dictionary as an indispensable reference book. It certainly belongs in any self-respecting library.

'Dr Pei's book is very readable; his style and his excellent choice of examples will delight his readers. Moreover, his philological views are, in general, correct—and such a happy state of affairs is rare in popular works on linguistics.'—*Birmingham Post*

'It would be difficult to imagine a more comprehensive and erudite yet readable analysis of the spoken and the written word viewed in every conceivable aspect.'—*John O'London's Weekly*

2nd Impression   Demy 8vo   25s. net

THE WORLD'S CHIEF LANGUAGES

The study of foreign languages has become a greater need than ever, but the ordinary man or woman needs other tools than those of high specialization. This volume therefore presents the main facts about languages not in the form of a philosophical or psychological or literary essay, not from the historical and scientific point of view, but as something of immediate practical value.

The author describes the world's main languages and their geographical distribution, the linguistic families and the elementary relationships among their members, the identification of the written and possibly the spoken form of several important tongues, and lastly the description of the sounds and grammatical structure, together with a selective vocabulary, of seven of the world's most widely-spoken languages.

The present volume is the third edition, revised, of a work first published under the title *Languages for War and Peace*.

3rd Impression   Demy 8vo   36s. net

GEORGE ALLEN AND UNWIN LTD